VISION 2000:

QUALITY AND OPPORTUNITY

THE FINAL REPORT OF VISION 2000

A REVIEW OF THE MANDATE

What should Ontario's college system look like in the year 2000
— and how do we get there from here?

Ministry of
Colleges and
Universities
Ontario

ISBN 0-7729-7207-9

Additional copies of this report are available from the:

Ontario Council of Regents,

790 Bay Street, 10th Floor,

Toronto, Ontario

M5G 1N8

(416) 965-4234

(416) 965-8441 (fax)

Le présent rapport est aussi publié en français

Ontario Council of Regents
for Colleges of
Applied Arts and Technology

Ontario

Conseil ontarien
des affaires
collégiales

10th Floor
790 Bay Street
Toronto, Ontario
M5G 1N8

10 e étage
790 rue Bay
Toronto (Ontario)
M5G 1N8

Office of the Chair

Bureau du président

(416)965-4234

May 11, 1990

The Honourable Sean Conway
Minister, Ministry of Colleges and Universities
22nd Floor, Mowat Block
Queen's Park
Toronto, Ontario

Dear Minister:

The Council of Regents is pleased to forward to you the final report of the Vision 2000 Steering Committee, **Vision 2000: Quality and Opportunity**. We are confident that the report's findings provide a significant point of departure for renewing the mandate of Ontario's college system.

Vision 2000 has been an experiment in collaboration, involving a wide range of stakeholders from the colleges and the wider community. This report provides substantial evidence that participation does inspire creativity and commitment.

The Council lends its voice to that of the Vision 2000 Steering Committee concerning the importance of a timely release of this report to stimulate further discussion. Council stands ready to respond directly to recommendations which deal with its role and to assist, when called upon, with other initiatives.

Council wishes to express its gratitude to you, Minister, and to your Deputy, Dr. Tom Brzustowski, for your leadership and sustained support. We also wish to thank the Honourable Lyn McLeod, former Minister of Colleges and Universities, who initiated Vision 2000.

Council owes a special note of thanks to the 33 members of the Steering Committee for their dedication and perseverance in bringing together in this final report the insights of students, faculty, support staff, administrators, boards of governors, unions and other groups and individuals. We are also grateful to Vision 2000's 106 hard-working study team members for their important contributions to the Steering Committee's deliberations.

Vision 2000 has posed a challenge for Ontario's colleges. It is the challenge of enhancing quality and opportunity so that the system can meet the needs of students and contribute to the economic and social goals of Ontario into the next century. The Council believes this is a goal well worth pursuing, and is convinced that, with your leadership, it will be achieved.

Sincerely,

Charles E. Pascal
Chair, Ontario Council of Regents

Table of Contents

Members of the Vision 2000 Steering Committee

Doug Auld,
President,
Loyalist College

John Evans,
Chair,
Allelix Biopharmaceuticals Inc.

Gaston Franklyn,
Vice President, Academic,
St. Clair College

Louise L. Gauthier,
Barrister & Solicitor,
Racicot, Bonney, Aube,
    Gauthier

Jay Jackson,
President, Local 245 of Ontario
    Public Service Employees
    Union, and
Technologist, Visual Arts,
    Sheridan College

Lorna Marsden,
Professor of Sociology,
University of Toronto, and
Senator, Toronto-Taddle Creek

Helen Burstyn,
Deputy Secretary,
Premier's Council Secretariat,
Government of Ontario

Andy Faas,
Executive Vice-President,
National Grocers Wholesale
    Services Group

Edith Garneau,
Chair, Ontario Federation of
    Students

Robert Gordon,
President,
Humber College

Bill Kuehnbaum,
President, Local 655 of Ontario
    Public Service Employees
    Union, and
Professor, Cambrian College

Kim McCulloch,
Vice-President, Professional
    Services,
Ontario Secondary School
    Teachers Federation

James Clancy,
President,
Ontario Public Service
    Employees Union

Nancy Forrester,
Professor,
Durham College

Ruth Gates,
Vice-President, Community
    Services,
Fanshawe College

Shirley Holloway,
Dean of Science and
    Technology,
George Brown College

Tony Manera,
Senior Vice President,
Canadian Broadcasting
    Corporation

Keith McIntyre,
President,
Mohawk College

continued ...

Riel Miller,
Manager, Policy and Research,
   Ontario Council of Regents,
and Executive Officer, Steering
   Committee

Viv Nelles,
Chair,
Ontario Council on University
   Affairs

Howard Rundle,
Vice-President, Academic,
Fanshawe College

Bob Siskind,
President,
Decade Developments

Jim Turk,
Director of Education,
Ontario Federation of Labour

Mary Morrison,
Chair,
Board of Governors,
Confederation College

Roy Olsen,
Chair,
Board of Governors,
St. Lawrence College

Brian Segal,
President,
University of Guelph

Jo Surich,
President,
Brocksway Information
   Technologies Inc.

George Wheball,
Chair, Ontario Community
   College Student Presidents'
   Association

Penny Moss,
Executive Director,
Ontario Public School Boards
   Association

Charles E. Pascal, (Chair)
Chair,
Ontario Council of Regents, and
Chair, Steering Committee

Bernard Shapiro,
Deputy Secretary of Cabinet,
Cabinet Office,
Government of Ontario

Christopher Trump,
Executive Director,
Association of Colleges of
   Applied Arts and Technology
   of Ontario

Tony Wilkinson,
President,
Lambton College

Vision 2000 acknowledges the following people who also served on the Steering Committee during earlier stages of the process:

Jeff Carew,
former Chair,
Ontario Community College Student Presidents'
   Association

Graham Collins,
former Executive Director,
Association of Colleges of Applied Arts and
   Technology of Ontario

Jim Head,
President,
Ontario Secondary School Teachers Federation

Shelly Potter,
former President,
Ontario Federation of Students

Glenna Carr,
former Deputy Minister,
Ministry of Skills Development

Marc Godbout,
former Chair,
Ontario Council for Franco-Ontarian
   Education

Trevor Lall,
former Chair,
Ontario Community College Student
   Presidents' Association

Acknowledgments

A project of this magnitude, with its comprehensive approach to collaboration, consultation and research, requires uncommon dedication and inspiration on the part of all participants. On behalf of the Vision 2000 Steering Committee, I would like to thank all those who contributed their time and wisdom to point the way for renewing Ontario's college system.

In particular, the Steering Committee owes a great deal to the Study Team Chairs: Howard Rundle, Lorna Marsden, Ruth Gates, Keith McIntyre and Penny Moss. Their personal commitment and inspirational leadership provide a practical example of how the colleges will realize a renewed mandate.

The Vision 2000 Steering Committee is especially grateful for the skill and dedication of Riel Miller, Manager, Policy and Research for the Council of Regents. He played a crucial role in devising the consultative and analytical approach adopted by Vision 2000. He was also a highly capable team leader, researcher, writer, and Executive Officer to both the Steering Committee and Study Team 2. His role in co-ordinating the project was key to its success.

The Council of Regent's Senior Policy Analyst, Brian Wolfe, contributed invaluable conceptual and analytical skills throughout the project. His comprehensive grasp of the system and his work as Executive Officer for Study Team 1, assistant to Study Team 5, researcher and writer, were a major contribution to the project.

The work of three study teams was made possible by the essential and distinctive contributions of five people we were fortunate to be able to second from the colleges. Francie Aspinall (Centennial), Harv Honsberger (Sheridan), and Starr Olsen (Humber) were the executive officers of Study Teams 3, 4 and 5 respectively. We are grateful for their tireless efforts to make sure all constituencies were heard in this process. We would also like to thank Terry Dance (George Brown) who served in the early stages of the process as the Executive Officer to Study Team 4, and Dugald McDonald (Fleming) who provided support and development in the initial phases of the project.

We extend our thanks to Norman Rowen who assisted with drafting this final report and was heavily involved in Study Team 4's research. We could not have completed this document without his in-depth knowledge of Ontario's college system, his strong analytical ability, and his commitment to teamwork.

We are very thankful for the immense dedication and top notch editorial, design and production skills brought to the project by Catherine Clement. As Communications Co-ordinator, she designed, edited and supervised the production of Vision 2000's publications, including our newsletter *Looking Forward*. She also designed this publication's cover and layout.

We are deeply indebted to Cheryl Hamilton for her ability to bring clarity to our ideas and make words come to life.

Appreciation is also extended to: Peter Adams (MPP Peterborough) who volunteered to interview a number of his fellow MPPs on their perceptions of the colleges; Phil Shaw who played a key role as our initial Communications Co-ordinator; Craig McFadyen who was our able research associate; and the many competent authors and researchers who produced Vision 2000's background papers which provide a solid base of information and analysis for future reference.

We also appreciate the effort of the many participants from different government ministries, including Ralph Benson and Peter Wright of the Ministry of Colleges and Universities who worked closely with the Vision 2000 Steering Committee.

Special thanks are owed to Michele Nugent. She provided sustained and effective logistical support from beginning to end. And last, but certainly not least, we wish to express our gratitude to the staff at the Council of Regents, Barb Lidston, Dana Boettger, Terry Pitre and Mora Thompson. They devoted many extra hours to ensuring that Vision 2000 ran smoothly.

Finally, to the many hundreds of Vision 2000 partners, whose ideas led the process, we thank you for making this your report.

Charles E. Pascal
Chair, Vision 2000 Steering Committee

Dedication

This report is dedicated to the memory of Norman A. Sisco who played a key role in the development of Ontario's colleges. We believe he would be pleased with Vision 2000 and its efforts to sustain his dream.

We also dedicate this report to future generations of lifelong learners with the hope that Vision 2000 will enhance their opportunities for high quality, career-oriented education.

1

Introduction:
The Vision 2000 Process

Vision is seeing beyond the immediacy of the day. It is understanding the temper of the times, the outlines of the future, and how to move from one to the other. Vision is seeing where life is headed, and how to make the transition from here to there most effectively. Vision is seeing what life could be like while dealing with life as it is. Vision is having some sense of the inner impulse of the Age. It is sensing what is felt, yet unarticulated, in the public soul and then giving it voice. Vision is seeing the potential purpose that's hidden in the chaos of the moment, yet which could bring to birth new possibilities for a people.

William Van Dusen Wishard
A World in Search of Meaning

In October 1988 a comprehensive and far-reaching review of Ontario's system of Colleges of Applied Arts and Technology was set in motion by then Minister of Colleges and Universities, the Honourable Lyn McLeod. The Council of Regents, a policy and planning agency which reports to the Minister, was asked to oversee the project and develop "a vision of the college system in the year 2000."

From the outset, it was vitally important that Vision 2000 be directed by a representative group of people who had a stake in the college system. The Vision 2000 Steering Committee was comprised of educators from colleges, schools and universities, students, employers, and labour and government representatives. The role of these 33 individuals was to guide the overall project.

A priority for Vision 2000 was the process of consultation. The Steering Committee felt that the best way to facilitate the process was to structure the review as several distinct inquiries. Five study teams were established to handle the work of research and public consultation, with each group focussing on a different aspect of the college system and on different constituencies.

Each study team was composed of a chair, who also sat on the Steering Committee, an executive officer who handled the day-to-day activities of the group, and a number of volunteers. The volunteers, or study team members, were representatives of the constituencies being consulted by that team. For example, representatives from business, industry and labour were members of the team that examined the economy. (For a listing of each study team's members, see Appendix A.)

The study teams were responsible for all facets of their investigation. In fact, due to the specific nature of each team's inquiry, the method of conducting research and consultation was customized for the specific constituencies being consulted. This flexible methodology provided the opportunity for these stakeholders to participate in not just the consultative process, but the analytical process as well.

The study teams were asked to report regularly to the Steering Committee. In the end, each submitted a final report with recommendations for consideration by the Steering Committee.

Study Team 1's task was to provide an empirical snapshot of the current college system and its external environment. The findings were to be used as background information by the other study teams.

Study Team 2 examined the economic role of the colleges. Specifically, the team investigated the changing nature of the economy, technology and the labour force.

Study Team 3's research was entitled "Colleges and the Communities." The concern of this group was to find ways the college system could promote access and educational support for Ontario's diverse student population, especially those learners or groups who had been traditionally underserved.

Study Team 4's investigation focussed on the challenges to individual colleges and the college system. In particular, the study team wanted to examine different organizational models for the college system, and explore the issues of quality, access, standards and curriculum.

Study Team 5's task was to examine the links between the colleges and other educational institutions, principally secondary schools and universities.

A special "sixth table" brought together the Francophone representatives from the five study teams, and representatives of the Ministry of Colleges and Universities and the Council for Franco-Ontarian Education. This group produced a discussion paper on a Francophone vision of Ontario's colleges.

In early 1989, Vision 2000 published *With the Future in Mind: An Environmental Scan* — a document which explored a number of assumptions and forecasts about the future of work, the economy, demographics and social trends, as well as data about the colleges. The publication was designed to stimulate discussion about the world in which the colleges will operate by the turn of the century. More importantly, it was presented to encourage people to begin the process of planning responses to that world.

Meanwhile, the five study teams were involved in an exciting process of research and consultation. Each study team commissioned a number of research papers designed to evoke discussion and debate.

In addition, each team solicited comments and ideas from a wide range of individuals and groups both inside and outside the college system. Meetings, focus groups and personal one-on-one interviews were conducted, and projects were initiated which requested information, attitudes and ideas; hundreds of submissions — termed "visions" — were received. Most of the visions were authored by people working in the colleges, but many were sent in by individuals and organizations outside the system. These consultations and submissions played an important part in the formulation of each team's policy recommendations.

To gain insight from the experience of others, Vision 2000 also reviewed some of the literature on major trends in college systems of other jurisdictions. The review included other parts of Canada, such as British Columbia, Alberta, Nova Scotia and Prince Edward Island, and other countries, such as the United States (particularly California, Florida, Iowa and Virginia), New Zealand and the United Kingdom. The college systems in other jurisdictions are not identical to Ontario's, but in many cases issues and directions for change are both similar and equally urgent.

While this research and consultation was taking place, Vision 2000 was also participating in other events in order to encourage participation and ideas. For example, presentations were made to the Ministers' Conference on Post-Secondary Education, the Select Committee on Education, the Deans of Arts of Ontario's universities, the Directors of Education, and the Association provinciale des cadres francophones des collèges communautaires de l'Ontario.

In addition, Vision 2000 sponsored a focus group with college alumni. And interviews were conducted with the Premier of Ontario, 13 Cabinet Ministers, the Leader of the Opposition and 30 Members of the Provincial Parliament (MPPs).

The purpose of these methods of data gathering was not only to provide information for Vision 2000's review; by actively involving a broad cross-section of stakeholders, Vision 2000 wanted to promote strategic thinking, collaboration, and partnerships in practice. The intent was to make the system better able to engage in this type of process and to provide impetus for continuing such activity.

The massive participation in this project, in and of itself, was an important landmark of co-operation for the college system.

The entire body of research and public consultation was summarized and published in Vision 2000's 39 background papers. Each study team produced a number of background documents. These papers were distributed for discussion purposes to the Steering Committee, and then to the colleges and interested members of the public. During the review, interested parties were kept updated on Vision 2000 through the project's regular bilingual newsletter, *Looking Forward*.

Between December 1989 and January 1990, the five study teams delivered their final reports to the Steering Committee. After considering the issues and recommendations brought forth by the study teams, the Steering Committee developed this final report Vision 2000: Quality and Opportunity. Interested readers may refer to the study team final reports and the background papers for specific sources and data, and for detailed results of Vision 2000's research and consultation. These reports and papers are listed in Appendix C.

It is important to note that the arguments and recommendations contained in this report represent the strong majority opinion of the Steering Committee. Where there were differences among members over the specifics of certain proposals, we have endeavoured to present the various viewpoints in the text. Some members of the Steering Committee participated in Vision 2000 as individuals, and some as representatives of particular organizations.

Members of the Steering Committee, the study teams and the hundreds of participants in the Vision 2000 process all agreed on the importance of the changes taking place, the critical nature of the challenges these social and economic changes present to Ontario, and the necessity of renewing the colleges as an indispensable part of our efforts to prosper in the future.

It is our hope that the directions offered will be the subject of continued discussion as we make the journey to the year 2000 and beyond.

2

The Need for Renewal

2.1 Preamble

Today, a quarter-century after its inception, the college system is at a crossroads. There is widespread concern among stakeholders that the system must undergo some fundamental changes in order to fulfil the career-education needs of individuals, communities and the economy in the 21st century. After 25 years, there is also a need to re-ignite the spirit which energized the early formative years of the colleges and which is needed again to take the system through a process of creative renewal.

While Vision 2000 is very much a forward-looking process, it is important to look back to see how the system came to this turning point and why. We must evaluate the many successes of the colleges, so that the system can build on its strengths; and assess what is in need of reform, so that the system can turn current challenges into future opportunities.

The need for renewal exists not only because of developments in the past, but also because of projections for the future. This is a time of unprecedented change in the social, political and economic environment in which the colleges operate. Ontario's colleges must adapt to the pressures for change, or be overtaken by them. The recommendations in this report are intended to enable the system to respond to these pressures in their next quarter-century of development.

This chapter begins with a review of the original mandate given to the colleges in the 1960s and the circumstances which surrounded the founding of the system. Next, there is a discussion of the new environment of the 1990s, particularly in relation to economic and demographic change in Ontario. Then we describe how the system has grown and developed since the 1960s. The final section looks at the major challenges facing the college system.

2.2 Founding of the Colleges

When Ontario's colleges were created 25 years ago, it was a time of massive growth and change in the educational system. The baby boom was engulfing the system: new schools and university facilities were being built at an unprecedented rate to accommodate the demand. Not only were there more children coming into the system than ever before, but students were staying in school longer. In addition to the pressures of expansion, school curricula were being overhauled, secondary school programs were being reorganized, and a host of new vocational schools were being built.

It was also the decade in which a human being first walked on the moon; scientific discovery and technological change were starting to accelerate, and a growing gap between the emerging needs of the economy and the skills available in the labour force was seen as a cause for concern. It was to the educational system that leaders turned to ensure that Ontario would have the skilled human resources it would need for the coming decades.

The Education Minister of the day, the Honourable William Davis, told the Legislature on May 21, 1965,[1] that Ontario was about to take a major step forward in the development of its educational system with the establishment of a "new level and type of education." The new system of community colleges would "above all else" help the government fulfil its promise to provide, through education and training, equality of opportunity for all and the fullest possible development of each individual's potential.

To that end, the colleges were directed to serve those parts of the population whose needs were not being met by the existing educational system. The colleges, which were to focus mainly on career-oriented education, would fill in the gap and create a system which would be "a coherent whole ... from kindergarten to the post-graduate level." They would serve secondary school graduates who were not university-bound, but who wanted to further their education beyond high school. And at a time when education was considered to be almost the exclusive purview of the young, the mandate of the colleges included meeting the needs of adults "at all socio-economic levels, of all kinds of interests and aptitudes, and at all stages of educational achievement."

Because these new colleges of applied arts and technology were being created as the "remaining section" of the educational system, and in order to differentiate their role, their mandate was expressed largely in terms of what they were not. Every college was given the responsibility to:

- provide courses of types and levels beyond, or not suited to, the secondary school setting;
- meet the needs of graduates from any secondary school program, apart from those wishing to attend university; and

---

[1] Ontario Department of Education, *Colleges of Applied Arts and Technology Basic Documents* (Toronto, Ontario Department of Education, June 1967), p. 5-16.

- meet the educational needs of adults and out-of-school youth, whether or not they were secondary school graduates.

Davis noted that these colleges were not designed to be universities by another name; they would not offer university-level courses in general or liberal education. Nor was there a need for Ontario's colleges to emulate those in other jurisdictions, such as the United States, which provided transfer or university-equivalent courses leading to advanced placement in universities. However, since qualified college students should not be prevented from attending university, a committee was planned to consider conditions and procedures under which universities would admit outstanding college graduates.

The Minister emphasized the vital role this new type of education should play in the economic and social development of Ontario. With knowledge, particularly in scientific areas, doubling every ten years, he said, a higher level of education was going to be required of everyone; knowledge workers, as opposed to manual workers, were going to be a prime economic need. Further, the rapid rate of technological innovation was threatening to overwhelm the capacity of the existing system, with its vocational centres and institutes of technology, to provide the level of skills training relevant to the needs of the economy. Davis said it was "essential to the continued growth and expansion of the economy of our Province, and of our nation, that adequate facilities be made generally available for the education and training of craftsmen, technicians and technologists."

The colleges were given a distinct community focus: "they will be designed to meet the needs of the local community." Programs could, and should, vary from one community to another; there would be a local board of governors for each college, and local program advisory committees in the various fields of study. The colleges were specifically charged with providing opportunities for learning in non-traditional ways. They were to accommodate part-time learners, offer evening as well as daytime classes, provide on-the-job or after-hours skills upgrading and updating for workers, and provide a wide variety of courses of varying lengths, including work-experience programs.

In 1967, 19 colleges opened their doors, built on the foundations of the existing technology institutes and vocational centres. That year, the government's *Basic Documents* enunciated four additional principles for the colleges:
- they must embrace total education, vocational and avocational, regardless of formal entrance qualifications, with provision for complete vertical and horizontal mobility;
- they must develop curricula that meet the combined cultural aspirations and occupational needs of the student;
- they must operate in the closest possible co-operation with business and industry, and with social and other public agencies, including education, to ensure that curricula are at all times abreast, if not in advance of the changing requirements of a technological society; and
- they must be dedicated to progress, through constant research, not only in curricula but in pedagogical technique and in administration.[2]

---

[2] Ibid., p. 32.

It was again emphasized that the new level of education should fit into the educational system as a coherent whole. A curriculum committee was proposed for each college, with representatives from the colleges, the universities and the secondary schools and chaired by a representative of industry, business or a public agency, to investigate how programs of study at the different educational levels could be integrated.

There was specific reference to some of the supports that colleges should provide. Assessment and counselling would be critical and college admission was to be based "on the ability profile of the student in a selected field of endeavour rather than on prescriptive entrance requirements alone," using diagnostic testing and personal interviews conducted by teams of counsellors. Upgrading programs "at and for all levels" were to be introduced, including academic upgrading for those who did not finish secondary school, language training for non-English-speaking new Canadians, and specialty courses to meet the specific requirements of a college program.

2.3 A New Environment

In many ways, the founding statement for the colleges in 1965 was prophetic. It predicted some of the major economic factors that would influence a college system providing career education in the 1990s: the enormous influence of new technology, the emergence of the "knowledge" worker in the age of information and communications, and the need for higher skill levels in the workforce. What the architects of the new system could not have foreseen was the pace and magnitude of change in the era of the global village and the silicon chip.

The environment of the 1990s is very different from the one in which the colleges were created, when the economy was dominated by manufacturing and the natural resource sector; the technological base was relatively stable; and production was becoming increasingly automated. At the beginning of the 1960s, population growth rates had reached an historic peak; the population was fairly homogeneous, mainly of European origin, and the traditional household was the nuclear family supported by a male breadwinner. There was a steadily expanding, youthful labour force, and most workers could expect to have one career last a lifetime.

The trends that were just beginning to take shape — and that helped to give rise to the creation of the college system — are in the process of transforming Ontario's economy a quarter of a century later. The demographics of the province are changing significantly, and the social priorities set at that time — the emphasis on equality of opportunity and the responsibility of the colleges to meet the needs of the wider community — have found new impetus in the realities of the 1990s.

Vision 2000's research and consultations have revealed that many aspects of the initial mission of the college system remain to be fulfilled. What is perhaps more significant for the future of the colleges is that the fundamental mandate on which the system was founded — to provide career education for high school graduates, to provide training opportunities for adult workers, and to serve a diversity of communities — has become even more important for Ontario in the 1990s.

Trends such as the aging of the workforce, industrial restructuring, technological innovation, and the changing skill content of jobs highlight the need for a dynamic college system which provides high-quality, relevant career education for a broad range of learners.

Ontario's workforce is undergoing some fundamental changes because of demographic trends. The growth rate of the population is slowing down. From 1921 to 1991, average growth per decade was about 19 per cent. In contrast, from 1991 to 2001, Ontario's population is projected to grow only 11.1 per cent and total growth in the following decade is projected to be about 7.9 per cent. Coinciding with the lower rate of population growth will be a fairly dramatic increase in the median age of Ontario's population. The median age is projected to rise from about 32 years at the close of the 1980s, to 40 years in 2011. Between 1987 and 2011 the population 45 years and over will grow by 81 per cent whereas the under 45 population will increase by only four per cent. By 2011 the first wave of the baby boom will have reached 65, and retirements will begin to affect the "skills bank" of the economy.

Chart 2.1

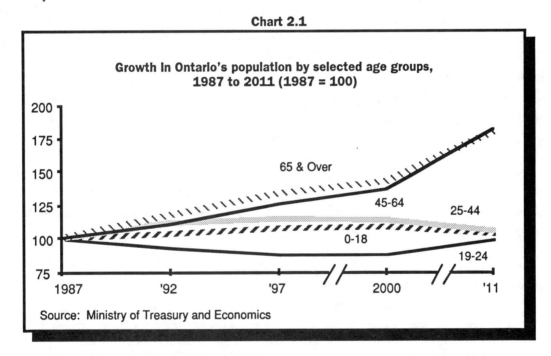

Growth in Ontario's population by selected age groups, 1987 to 2011 (1987 = 100)

Source: Ministry of Treasury and Economics

As the supply of young entrants to the labour force declines, the province is shifting from labour surpluses and a relatively young workforce, to increasing labour shortages in a number of sectors and a "greying" workforce. Critical labour shortages in some industrial fields are already occurring, but at the same time there is unemployment in others, mainly among lower-skilled and older workers. This is occurring at a time when increased competition on a global scale, and the race to keep up with the latest technological innovations are forcing industrialized economies around the world not only to "retool" their factories, plants and offices, but also to retrain their workers. The ability to adapt quickly to new technology and other changes in the marketplace has become a major challenge for employers and employees alike.

Many traditional manufacturing industries are undergoing difficult adjustments in this new environment. Success in many industries is no longer predicated on mass production of a single product, but customized production of products geared to the specific needs of the client. The assembly line is being replaced by multiskilled teams, quality circles and other new-style work environments. Many employers are emphasizing the need for workers who can think critically, communicate well, and work with others in solving problems.

The service sector has become the fastest growing sector of the economy. However, many service jobs continue to be dependent on the goods-producing sector. Many of the high-growth service occupations are low-skill and low-paying, with limited prospects for promotion. On the other hand, the service sector is also creating a whole range of new highly-skilled professional-level occupations, in finance, communications and other fields.

Most of the workers in Ontario who will be required to adapt to new technologies, economic restructuring and increased global competition in the year 2000 are already in the labour market. Many of these adult workers will need retraining not just once, but several times in the course of their working lives.

Canadian employers have tended to exhibit significantly lower rates of investment in training than many of this nation's major trading competitors. In the past, employers have been able to import skills from outside Canada to compensate for skills shortages. But the supply-demand disparity in skilled occupations is also being experienced in other industrialized countries; it is not expected, therefore, that immigration will provide the solution. Canada, and Ontario, will have to train — and retrain — their own.

The Premier's Council on Technology has made it eminently clear that workforce training is crucial to the future prosperity of Ontario. "Those economies that have invested in the basic and advanced skills of their workforces have achieved stronger economic performance through superior worker training and labour market responsiveness."[3]

The Economic Council of Canada, in its recent report *Good Jobs Bad Jobs*, also conveyed the urgency of the economic challenge for governments, educational institutions and employers:

> In the emerging economy, universal attainment of basic skills, the development of excellence through highly qualified personnel, and widespread access to retraining opportunities are becoming imperative. To meet the challenges of the global marketplace and the economic expectations of its people, Canada simply must be a world leader with respect to the quality of its work force. This will require fundamental changes in the country's commitment and approach to education and training.[4]

The Economic Council makes the case that Canada must provide not only advanced training to produce highly qualified personnel, but also basic skills training for a wide range of underqualified

---

[3] Premier's Council, *Competing in the New Global Economy, Report of the Premier's Council*, Vol. 1 (Toronto: Queen's Printer for Ontario, 1988), p. 215.

[4] Economic Council of Canada, *Good Jobs Bad Jobs*, Employment in the Service Economy (Ottawa: Ministry of Supply and Services, 1990), p. 1.

workers, and adjustment training for those whose skills no longer match the demands of the marketplace. The Council warns of a growing segmentation and polarization in terms of earnings, the skill content of jobs, job stability, and the location of employment. Employment problems facing poorly educated and displaced workers appear to be growing, at the same time as the job market for highly skilled, well-paid, stable occupations is expanding.

Economic trends are not the only forces for change in the new environment; Ontario is changing in other ways. We have become an increasingly multicultural society; fewer immigrants now come from Europe, and more from the nations of Asia, Africa and Central and South America. Many new immigrants require language training before they can participate in education or work, and many come from countries which do not have highly developed educational and training opportunities. Those who do have qualifications for professional and technical jobs in Ontario find it difficult to get their credentials validated here. People from other cultures want to be assured that their customs and heritage are respected, and that they will have an equal opportunity to succeed.

The role of women has changed. Women now make up 45 per cent of the provincial labour force, and their participation rate continues to increase; however, they continue to earn, on average, only two-thirds of what men earn. Women are also underrepresented in many of the occupations that are experiencing critical labour shortages. Many women need support services, particularly child care, to enable them to take advantage of available training opportunities. Other groups, such as persons with disabilities, want better access to education and the labour force so that they, too, can realize their potential.

Demographics may also affect the colleges in future in a more indirect way, through the government's ability to pay for post-secondary education. The government expenditure dependency index (see Chart 2.2 below) will rise in the decades ahead. The aging population means that a greater proportion of public resources will likely need to be devoted to the health sector.

Together, the economic and social changes in Ontario are putting new pressures on the colleges. While the colleges have filled a much-needed role in career education in the last 25 years, they are being challenged to update their mandate in order to remain relevant to the real needs of the province and its people.

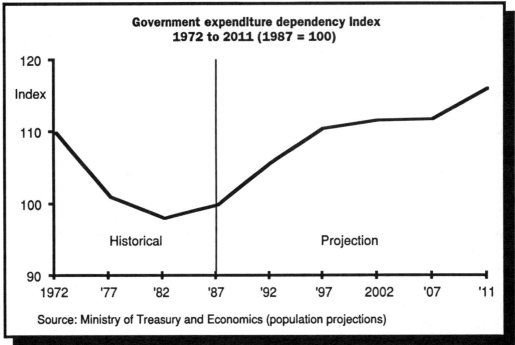

Chart 2.2

Government expenditure dependency index
1972 to 2011 (1987 = 100)

Index

Historical   Projection

1972   '77   '82   '87   '92   '97   2002   '07   '11

Source: Ministry of Treasury and Economics (population projections)

Note: This chart shows, in index form, the ratio of the dependent population (0-14, and 65 and over) to the working age population (15-64) in Ontario. In estimating the dependent population, the senior population has been adjusted upward by a factor of 2.5, to take into account that, on a per capita basis, the cost of public services to seniors exceeds the cost of services to those under 14. This adjusted figure has been added to the youth population to create a measure of the dependent population in public expenditure terms. The adjustment factor of 2.5 is consistent with values determined in Canadian and American studies in the 1970s.

2.4 Evolution of the System

The colleges have more than met initial expectations in providing career-oriented post-secondary education for the "tidal waves" of students who began pouring out of the secondary schools in the 1960s. Five years after the first colleges opened, there were over 35,000 students enrolled in full-time post-secondary programs; today, there are over 95,000.

The creation of a new level of education across the province in the span of a few short years was a considerable accomplishment. Today, the system has 22 colleges, offering programs on more than 100 campuses in over 60 cities and towns across the province. A 23rd institution, the French-language college, La Cité collégiale, is opening its doors to students in the fall of 1990.

In addition to the 95,000 full-time post-secondary students, there are approximately 70,000 students enrolled in full-time, non-post-secondary training programs (apprenticeships and adult training programs of short duration). There are also an estimated 560,000 students, most of whom are adults over age 25, taking part-time, mainly career-oriented studies.

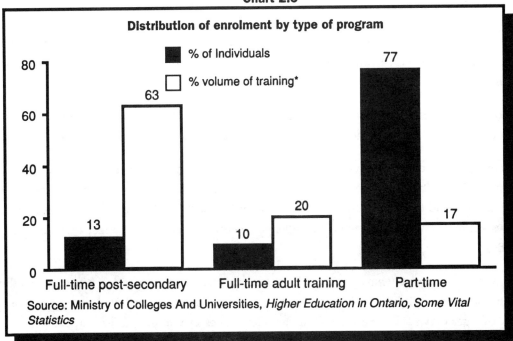

Chart 2.3

Distribution of enrolment by type of program

- ■ % of Individuals
- □ % volume of training*

Full-time post-secondary: 13, 63
Full-time adult training: 10, 20
Part-time: 77, 17

Source: Ministry of Colleges And Universities, *Higher Education in Ontario, Some Vital Statistics*

*% when number of individuals is converted to full-time equivalents.

In a given year, about one in ten Ontarians aged 17 and older is taking a course at a college. As an illustration of the magnitude of more recent growth in the system, between 1978 and 1987 college enrolments in full-time, post-secondary programs rose by 48 per cent, and in part-time courses by 44 per cent.

As anticipated in the original mandate, the colleges provide a variety of occupation-oriented courses and programs, ranging from training in the trades to three-year diploma programs, such as nursing and engineering technology. They have also responded to the need for basic education, such as life skills and literacy, for adults. In addition to the broad range of career programs, the colleges also provide many general interest and personal development courses.

The colleges have taken the breadth of their mandate to heart. Learners may go to college today to learn to read, to fly a helicopter, to dance, to operate heavy equipment or to program a robot.

The colleges serve students with diverse educational achievements, racial and cultural backgrounds, ages and labour market status. Colleges have endeavoured to meet various special needs of students, and some have developed specific access initiatives. Through multiple campuses and development of distance education programs, particularly in Northern Ontario, the colleges have tried to become as geographically accessible as possible.

Colleges represent a valuable public resource in their communities. Most colleges are visibly engaged in community life, both institutionally (e.g. sponsoring public interest events, involvement in community causes like the United Way, hosting community debates on child care or student housing) and through the personal involvement of staff, some of whom hold political office or sit on local boards and agencies. The college campus in smaller communities, particularly in more rural parts of the province and in the North, is one of the major focal points, and is sometimes *the* major focus for community activities. In the large metropolitan centres, a number of colleges have formed successful partnerships with a variety of diverse cultural communities in an effort to identify and meet their needs.

In recognition of this country's dual linguistic heritage, there are French-language programs at a number of colleges. The new Francophone college, La Cité collégiale, will serve Eastern Ontario.

The colleges have coped with incredible rates of growth and development since they were established in the 1960s. In many ways, they had to learn from experience, because they were breaking new ground in Ontario. The province did not follow the U.S. model of junior colleges; the college system here was designed to be a parallel post-secondary sector, not a feeder system for the universities.

That distinctiveness may have inhibited links with the university sector, but it has helped the colleges to establish a unique place for career education in Ontario's educational spectrum. And while the colleges may not have achieved the same level of esteem in the public mind as the universities, they have made significant steps in this regard. In fact, other jurisdictions have used the college experience in this province as a model for the development of their own college systems.

Those who inaugurated the system intended that the colleges would have a substantial impact on Ontario's skilled labour force. And indeed the colleges have had a significant impact. In excess of 25,000 students now graduate annually from the colleges' one-, two- and three-year, post-secondary programs. About 7,000 complete programs in the applied arts (e.g. early childhood education, broadcasting and fashion arts). Another 8,000 graduate in business-related fields, including business and office administration. The health sciences annually graduate about 5,000 students. And another 5,000 complete technology programs, such as aviation technology, computer science, biochemical technology and electromechanical technology. In addition, about 7,000 apprentices complete their programs each year, most of whom will have attended college at some point during their apprenticeship and another 20,000 to 30,000 individuals complete adult training programs annually. The colleges are playing a key and significant role throughout the province in meeting Ontario's labour force requirements.

Where the colleges have seen opportunities to respond to changes in the marketplace, they have done so. For example, they developed a range of programs related to hospitality and tourism when they saw this was a major growth area in the service sector. They have continued to adapt to the information age by introducing computers both to the curriculum and the operation of their institutions.

The colleges have much in common across the province, but they have also had the autonomy to develop their own character and areas of specialization; two of many examples are the Lindsay natural resources campus of Sir Sandford Fleming College and the internationally recognized animation program at Sheridan College in Oakville.

Overall, the colleges have been responsive to the changing demands placed on them by governments and society at large. Whenever a program had to be mounted to meet a short- or longer-term economic or social priority — to meet a sudden surge in youth unemployment or to encourage women to enter non-traditional trades, for instance — the colleges have responded with innovative programs.

Adapting to the changing priorities of government has not been easy. Over the years, the colleges have met demands for a variety of short-term training courses purchased for a wide range of student needs by the federal Canada Employment and Immigration Commission (CEIC) and the provincial Ministry of Skills Development (MSD). Often, the training purchased by these agencies has been an unstable source of revenue, a problem compounded by the fact that colleges must regularly scramble to put together programs on short notice. Currently, these two funding sources provide almost 25 per cent of college operating revenues system-wide.

When the federal government introduced the Canadian Jobs Strategy (CJS) in 1985, there was a fundamental shift toward greater emphasis on the private sector in the development and delivery of training. MSD, which was created in 1985, has offset some of the shortfall in the colleges created by the federal policy changes, with programs such as Ontario Basic Skills and Transitions. Nevertheless, the lack of planning and co-ordination in the development of federal and provincial training and employment policies has had an adverse impact on the colleges' ability to plan and adapt.

Over the last 25 years, the colleges also have had to live with cyclical fluctuations in funding provided by the Ministry of Colleges and Universities (MCU), their major funder. When the colleges were formed, the province was expanding public services and facilities. But beginning in the mid- to late-1970s and continuing through to the mid-1980s, the colleges had to cope with high enrolment growth during a period of government restraint.

2.5 The Challenge to Change

Vision 2000 believes that the colleges have many accomplishments of which to be proud. However, we also recognize that there are problems in the system that need to be addressed as part of the process of renewal for the year 2000 and beyond. The following describes the major challenges facing the colleges. Each is discussed in greater detail later in this report.

Lack of system-wide standards and planning: There was an expectation in the original mandate that the colleges would operate as a system. There could be program variations from community to community to serve local needs, but the colleges were to be, in the words of the founding statement, "a province-wide system, carefully planned in its development."

However, there is widespread criticism that there are many similarly titled post-secondary programs across the system which do not yield the same qualifications or skills for those who graduate. This is a particular concern for employers who are hiring graduates, but it is also an impediment to student mobility across the college system. The pressure and support for more system-wide consistency in program outcomes is strong.

Significantly, the system currently has no means to either prove or disprove the perception that program variations indicate not only local adaptations, but differences in program quality. If the colleges are to be in a position to respond to the growing needs for career education in the 21st century, the system must be able to guarantee that its programs are of high quality.

There is also a need for more systematic planning across the system. Sound local planning should be based on shared information from colleges across the province. If there is a challenge which affects most or all colleges, such as student attrition, there should be some way for colleges to address it collectively. For example, groups of colleges might try different initiatives and report on their success. Further, specialized resources and expertise could be shared through more collaborative planning.

Insufficient general and generic education: In the four principles for the colleges outlined in 1967, colleges were directed to "embrace total education." But from the beginning of the college system, general education (e.g. studies in sociology, world events or the environment) has received less emphasis than vocational skills training in college post-secondary programming, and its position has further declined in the last decade. When funding restraints squeezed college budgets in the late 1970s, program hours were cut back, and the major casualty was general education. General education is supposed to constitute at least 30 per cent of post-secondary program content; however, most programs have considerably less.

The rapid pace of change in the workplace, particularly that caused by new technologies, has increased the need for students to acquire generic skills — such as problem-solving and critical thinking, as well as basic literacy, numeracy and computer literacy — so that they can learn new skills or adapt old ones. A worker who does not have the transferable skills to advance to better positions in his or her field may become trapped in a particular job. An over-concentration in many college programs on narrow occupation-specific skills, to the detriment of generic skills and general education, is restricting career opportunities for some college graduates and affecting the ability of business and industry to adapt quickly to the demands of the marketplace.

A greater emphasis in college programs on skills and knowledge that have broad applicability to different current and future uses is needed to serve the interests of Ontario's economy and society. If the diffusion of new technology is dependent on a broadly educated and skilled population, it is important to ensure that as many people as possible have technological literacy and other skills which are transferable to other jobs and occupations. These skills are not a substitute for job-specific skills, but are complementary to them. Moreover, general education and generic skills are important tools for good citizenship and help people cope with change in all aspects of their lives.

Limitations on access: The new environment demands that Ontario's colleges encourage greater participation in education and training by those in our society who are employment disadvantaged, such as the estimated one-sixth of the adult population who are functionally illiterate, the 30 per cent of high school students who drop out before receiving their graduation diploma, the growing numbers of older workers who are displaced by structural changes in the economy or technological innovation, and other groups which have traditionally been underserved by the educational system.

In 1965, the Education Minister indicated that colleges should serve their local communities. The growing diversity of communities, and particularly the multicultural face of Ontario, is placing increased demands on the colleges to improve accessibility for special communities. For some disadvantaged groups — such as those living in poverty, persons with physical disabilities, single parents, members of minority groups who speak neither English nor French, aboriginal peoples and those who are functionally illiterate — more active intervention is necessary to provide equitable access. Similar efforts are required for the colleges to play a full role in helping Ontario overcome the labour market inequality facing women and other groups. Without active promotion of equitable access, systemic barriers in the system will continue to put appropriate opportunities for educational and skills training beyond the reach of many.

The original mandate of the colleges anticipated that they would offer a range of upgrading programs for all levels of students. Most colleges are already engaged in providing preparatory or remedial programs for underprepared high school graduates; adult basic education programs, such as literacy training and basic skills training; English as a Second Language training; and other types of upgrading programs. However, the needs far surpass both the supply of programs and the available funding. If colleges are to enhance opportunities for the access and success of more students, the availability of preparatory, literacy, language and other such programs will have to be increased.

Inattention to adult part-time learners: The primary orientation of college institutional structures and the provincial funding formula is toward the full-time, post-secondary student who usually has just graduated from high school. This bias makes it difficult for colleges to provide the flexible programs and access services needed by the growing numbers of adult part-time learners, who are coming back to the educational system after some time in the workforce, and who now outnumber full-time post-secondary students by almost six to one.

The colleges are seen to have relegated the part-time learner to a peripheral position. The part-time student, who often has work and family responsibilities, does not have the variety of course selection or range of support services that are routinely available to the full-time student.

Adult learners who have been away from the educational system for years or who have educational credentials from outside Ontario often have difficulty getting recognition for the knowledge and skills they have acquired prior to enrolling in a college program. There is no accessible and equitable system of evaluating the prior learning and experience of entrants to college. Fair recognition of prior learning and experience is particularly important in encouraging adults to update existing skills or learn new ones.

Specific concerns from employers: The system is being challenged to work more effectively with employers in provision of fee-for-service training. Colleges were directed in the founding documents to co-operate closely with employers to ensure college curricula continued to be relevant and current to the marketplace. Employers in the past were mostly interested in hiring job-ready graduates, and the colleges have endeavoured to meet this demand. Today, employers are looking less for a college graduate with made-to-measure skills and more for one who understands technology, can adapt it and can learn new skills on the job. A number of employers are saying that many college programs do not give students those necessary skills.

The colleges have maintained links with a wide range of employers through program advisory committees and through other formal and informal ties. In addition, employer-sponsored training is accounting for a growing, although still small, share of system-wide college revenues (less than three per cent). Employers indicate there is much room for increased college participation in the delivery of employer-sponsored training. However, they stress that it will be necessary for colleges to become more knowledgeable about employer needs, place more emphasis on standards, be more flexible in curriculum design and location of training, and do more marketing of their training capabilities to the private sector.

Attrition: The need for more success strategies in the colleges is evidenced in an average attrition rate in college post-secondary programs of over 40 per cent. Students drop out for a variety of reasons, not all of them related to lack of success in their chosen college program, and the percentage is not out of line with the experience in other educational jurisdictions. However, a study by the Association of Colleges of Applied Arts and Technology of Ontario (ACAATO) identified student academic underpreparedness as a key factor in dropping out. Another study found that the characteristics of the academic environment of the college were particularly important in promoting student persistence.[5] The findings of the latter study also suggested that the level of preparedness may be related, in some cases, to academic achievement and, in others, to the choices students make about careers and post-secondary programs.

The original mandate of the colleges indicated that student assessment and counselling were critical. Currently, there is wide variation from college to college in assessment and counselling services. These services, provided at the time of admission and when necessary throughout the student's time in college, must be improved if the system is to address the problem of the "revolving door."

Missing links: A legacy of inaction in the past has resulted in relationships between educational institutions that feature more walls than doors.

The original college mandate specified that the colleges were to fit into the educational spectrum as part of a coherent whole. However, the joint schools-colleges-universities curriculum committees that were to foster links between the three sectors were never implemented. Individual institutions have made efforts to forge links with other educational bodies, but until recently there has been little in the way of provincial initiatives in this area.

---

[5] Peter Dietsche, "Describing and Predicting Freshman Attrition in a College of Applied Arts and Technology of Ontario," an unpublished doctoral thesis (Toronto: Ontario Institute for Studies in Education, 1988).

Better links between the schools and colleges are needed to smooth the transition for high school graduates entering college programs, to increase participation and to help ensure that students have an opportunity to succeed. The difficulty many high school graduates experience in college programs is often cited as a criticism of the secondary schools. However, given the mandate of the colleges to serve all high school graduates who are not going to university, this may equally be considered a shortcoming of the college system.

Trends in employment suggest the need for greater opportunities for college students to take advanced studies, either through improved college-university links or at the colleges. Advanced training opportunities will be particularly important in new technologies and other emerging sectors of the economy.

Development of human resources, curriculum and delivery methods: A system which is geared to providing up-to-date training for its students must have a faculty which is familiar with the latest developments in the workplace. In addition, a system which reaches many adult learners from a variety of backgrounds and experiences needs faculty, support staff and administrators trained to meet their needs, which will likely be quite different from the needs of the 18-year-old just out of high school. While some colleges provide effective professional development, there has been a general tendency to treat it as an individual rather than an institutional or system responsibility.

To begin to address this problem, in 1987 the Council of Presidents (formerly the Committee of Presidents) appointed a task force on "Human Resources in the Third Decade." The task force's recommendations were accepted in 1989, and modest funds have been pledged for implementation. However, there remain concerns about how to ensure that adequate funds are designated (and protected) in each college for the necessary ongoing development of staff and to ensure participation by faculty, as well as management, in implementation.

Human resource development will become even more important in future as large numbers of experienced teachers and administrators reach retirement age around the turn of the century.

In addition to highlighting the need for teacher training, the original mandate referred to colleges performing research in curriculum, pedagogical techniques and administration, and suggested a role for the colleges in co-operative curriculum development with industry. But the college system has not systematically engaged to any great extent in such studies.

Quality-access-funding trade-offs: The report of the Instructional Assignment Review Committee (IARC) in July 1985 identified adverse impacts on the colleges of the combination of huge enrolment growth (almost 50 per cent) and a substantial decline (33 per cent) in the real funding per student provided by MCU over the period 1978/79 to 1983/84. The committee said the colleges had been under enormous pressure to increase efficiency and had made significant gains.

> [However] we question ... whether perhaps these gains have been achieved at too great a cost in terms of educational quality, faculty and student morale, and institutional vitality. The excessive preoccupation with efficiency, almost to the

exclusion of any other social or educational values, may be threatening the viability of the college system."[6]

Many of those working in the colleges (both labour and management) told Vision 2000 that problems identified by IARC persist — problems pertaining to quality of education, faculty, staff and student morale, and institutional vitality. Based on our consultations with a broad range of stakeholders, we believe these problems persist because there is confusion about what the colleges should be doing — or what the provincial government wants them to be doing — and because the system continues to be preoccupied with cost-cutting and funding constraints.

The complexity of these issues, particularly the trade-offs between quality, access and funding, will be even greater in the 1990s. Enrolment projections prepared for Vision 2000 indicate the colleges should expect substantial growth in the years ahead. Thus the system will continue to face the challenge of meeting increasing demand for places and providing quality career education, within available public resources.

Chart 2.4

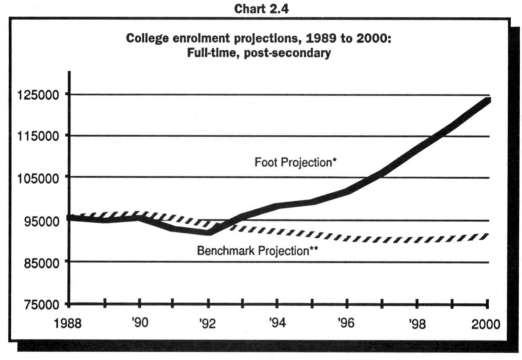

College enrolment projections, 1989 to 2000: Full-time, post-secondary

*The Foot Projection is based on an analysis of the impact on college participation rates of changes in variables such as per capita income, unemployment rates, and fees. For details see D. Foot and M. MacNiven, "The Determinants of Enrolment Rates and Enrolments in Ontario Community Colleges" in *Empirical Features of the College System. Background Papers* (Toronto: Ontario Council of Regents, 1990).
**The Benchmark Projection assumes that age-specific participation rates will remain at current levels (i.e. 1988 levels) throughout the projection period and thus reflects solely the impact of changing demographics.

---

[6] Instructional Assignment Review Committee, *Survival or Excellence? A Study of Instructional Assignment in Ontario Colleges of Applied Arts and Technology* (Toronto: Ministry of Colleges and Universities, July 1985), p. 9.

The Foot projections, shown in Chart 2.4, are presented with the caution that they depend on certain assumptions about growth in the economy and per capita incomes, and the ability of the colleges to respond to the needs of older (over 25) learners. The projections indicate that full-time post-secondary enrolment will be about 30 per cent higher in the year 2000 than in 1988. Increases in part-time enrolment are likely to be even greater. Even though the traditional source of full-time, post-secondary enrolment — the 17-to-24 age group — will decline in the 1990s, anticipated increases in participation rates among both youth and adults will fuel enrolment growth if colleges are prepared to meet their needs.

Competition for public resources among government services is not expected to diminish in the years ahead. Vision 2000 was urged to call for additional across-the-board funding for the colleges. We rejected this approach as simplistic and inadequate to the policy challenges facing Ontario today. Instead, this report attempts to identify key areas where we believe change and, in certain circumstances, additional funding are necessary. In particular, we emphasize the importance of clearly identifying and responding to the trade-offs between quality, access and funding. Vision 2000 does believe that it is crucial to introduce greater stability and clarity into college funding.

Labour-management relations: It should be noted that IARC was appointed to investigate the dispute over workload that was at the centre of the 1984 faculty strike. Although some changes were made pursuant to that report, labour-management relations cannot be said to have improved substantially since then. During the Vision 2000 process, there was another faculty strike, in 1989. It is a credit to all those engaged in Vision 2000 that the one-month work stoppage only slowed the process down and did not fundamentally alter the commitment to partnership.

The strike which occurred late in 1989 rekindled debate about the collective bargaining process. Opinions are sharply divided: generally, union leaders prefer a centralized bargaining process, while the Council of Presidents (COP) favours local bargaining. Vision 2000 is aware of the importance and sensitivity of this issue. It has already been the subject of an in-depth review, *The Report of the Colleges Collective Bargaining Commission,*[7] and was consequently not raised as a major issue during our consultations.

Members of the Steering Committee did discuss the status of labour-management relations toward the end of the Vision 2000 process, and were divided on the issue of local versus central forms of collective bargaining. However, given that the Minister and the college system are currently engaged, through forums other than Vision 2000, in detailed discussion of labour-management relations, the Steering Committee is confident there will be a full airing of views.

It is the shared concern of those involved in the Vision 2000 process that labour-management issues not be allowed to fester, thus jeopardizing the renewal of the system. Labour, management and government must deal constructively with these challenges.

---

[7] Colleges Collective Bargaining Commission, *The Report of the Colleges Collective Bargaining Commission* (Toronto: Ministry of Colleges and Universities, January 1988). The commission reported there was consensus at that time on keeping centralized bargaining, but with some improvements to the centralized process.

The foregoing discussion indicates that there are a number of significant areas in which the colleges face major challenges. At the same time, it is evident that the colleges have made and must continue to make a major contribution to career education and training in Ontario.

There are hundreds of thousands of former college students who have built successful careers based on the education, training and encouragement they received at college. There are thousands of employers, large and small, who have built profitable and productive enterprises with college-educated employees. And there are thousands of individuals in the colleges who have provided dedicated service to students and Ontario's communities. Moreover, many of the challenges facing the system are not all of the colleges' own making. Colleges have been buffeted by changing government policies and changing social and economic demands.

The winds of change are not likely to abate or to become more predictable in the years ahead. The educational needs of Ontario society are expected to increase in the future. The government and the colleges have the responsibility and an opportunity to respond to those needs.

3

A Renewed Mandate

3.1 Preamble

Vision 2000 was directed at the outset of this process to bring forward a vision of the college system in the year 2000. This meant developing a consensus around the major initiatives that stakeholders, both inside and outside the system, considered to be priorities for the coming decade. It also meant considering whether the mandate or mission of the system should be changed from that originally set out in the founding documents in the 1960s.

This chapter discusses the major objectives for change in the college system and proposes a renewed mandate for the future. It highlights the priorities for realizing the mandate and provides a brief outline of the rest of the report.

3.2 Quality and Opportunity

The renewed mandate and priorities for change proposed by Vision 2000 reflect our desire to realize two important objectives: *assuring quality* and *enhancing opportunity*. These two overriding objectives emerged from our assessment of both the colleges' past record and, more importantly, the new challenges facing Ontario.

As governments around the world grapple with the challenges of changing economic and social circumstances, education has re-emerged as one of the pre-eminent tools of public policy. The Organisation for Economic Co-operation and Development expressed this point clearly:

> Advanced economies must carefully appraise the content, funding and provision of both education and job training in order to promote a continuing learning process — the key not only to successful utilization of human resources and effective innovation

---

in the economy, but also to job security, career prospects, meaningful activity and personal development for the individual.[8]

Vision 2000 has concentrated on how to make the college system more effective. Assuring the quality of college education and enhancing the opportunity to participate will improve Ontario's chances of maintaining a prosperous and healthy society.

The message from employers, labour, the community and academic researchers is clear. Colleges are a pivotal component of the solution to many of our labour market and citizenship challenges. But in order for the college system to be part of the solution, not part of the problem, government leadership is essential.

We urge the government to take the initiatives outlined by Vision 2000 as a way of revitalizing the colleges. Like many organizations, from corporations and trade unions to hospitals and government ministries, colleges will find that the real challenge is to work smarter. Doing a better job at building a car, securing workers' jobs, treating patients, or delivering social services is what quality and opportunity are all about.

Assuring quality: The colleges must be able to assure the quality and consistency of educational attainments across the system. A college education must enhance students' ability to acquire information, reason clearly, think critically, communicate effectively, apply their knowledge and participate in society as informed and productive citizens.

As public educational institutions, the colleges have an obligation to provide a high standard of education which offers students more than narrow job-specific skills. A college education should be developmental in that it should provide a strong foundation for the student to continue learning. There is a qualitative difference between learning a technology and learning how to operate a particular machine. Learning *only* the latter can severely limit employment because the skills required in many occupations are changing rapidly. Developing students' abilities to analyze and apply knowledge, and providing them with skills that are generic rather than exclusively job-specific, will help them adapt to change.

Vision 2000 believes that quality assurance in the college system must mean not only that there are standards of excellence governing what a college credential stands for across Ontario, but also that the knowledge and skills students gain from a college education are those that help them to be contributing members of the workforce and of society in general.

A college education must be portable in the sense that for the student it opens doors that lead to further opportunities — in college, in other educational institutions, or in the workplace.

Enhancing opportunity: A college education should be accessible. Accessibility should include the opportunity to succeed, as well as the opportunity to enrol, and it must be provided in an

---

8 Organisation for Economic Co-operation and Development, *New Technologies in the 1990s: A Socio-economic Strategy* (Paris: OECD, 1988).

---

equitable manner. Access with success means that all students should have a reasonable chance to complete an appropriate college program. It means that access must go beyond providing an open door; after enrolment, there must be a supportive learning environment and a variety of strategies to help students succeed in college.

The colleges of the 1990s and beyond should strive to increase participation by groups that traditionally have been underserved by the educational system. Our economy and our society needs people who are skilled and who are able to continue learning during their entire life; the colleges are well positioned to provide those opportunities.

In a society as diverse as Ontario's, it is important that opportunities for learning in college be equally varied. The colleges of the future need to transform themselves to ensure that the needs of the adult, part-time learner, who has work and family responsibilities, are addressed. Accommodating diversity entails a whole range of activities, including promoting respect for human rights and cultural integrity, and fostering institutional adaptations to suit the requirements of students with special needs.

3.3 A Mandate for the Future

Ontario has made a substantial investment in the college system over the last two and a half decades. It is important that the colleges remain relevant to the needs of their communities as times change, and that, as public institutions, they continue to serve the educational needs of society as a whole.

The colleges have played a valuable role in career education and training over the last 25 years in Ontario. They fill a unique niche in the educational system. They are an alternative to university for students seeking education beyond secondary school. More than any other educational institution in the province, they serve the needs of adult learners, who have a variety of educational achievements and aspirations. They are the public institutions that employers and governments turn to for the training of workers.

There are those who argue that the colleges should pull back from the broad mandate they were given 25 years ago, from their current diversity of roles and clients, and concentrate on a more restricted set of needs and a narrower client focus. They argue that it is too difficult to perform a range of functions well, particularly in the fast-paced world in which we live today.

The system has had difficulty, at times, coping with the competing priorities entailed by a broad range of functions. However, these problems do not stem from an inherent inability of the colleges to manage a range of roles. Rather, the colleges have been buffeted by a number of factors unrelated to the exclusivity of focus or lack thereof. These other factors have been largely out of the control of the colleges — the impact of volatile government funding over the past decade; the lack of co-ordination of new initiatives affecting the colleges; the lack of involvement of the colleges in the planning for these initiatives; and the government's long hesitation in providing a positive and renewed mandate for the college system.

We also argue that the diverse and growing educational needs of Ontario are a compelling reason to maintain the broad mandate of the colleges so that colleges may be able to respond to the needs of the future — the needs of learners, employers and the larger community — as those needs evolve.

There was, perhaps surprisingly, little support during Vision 2000's extensive consultations and discussions for the view that the colleges should become more exclusive organizations. If anything, the consensus was that they should be more inclusive — they should be making greater efforts to serve those groups which have been least well served in the past. And, like so many institutions in our society today, colleges should be working to provide specific services tailored to meet distinct client needs. For the colleges, this translates into a learner-driven approach.

The original vision of the colleges contained in the founding documents looked to the colleges to be accessible, responsive, innovative and community-focussed. Vision 2000 has concluded that the colleges should become even more accessible, more needs-driven, more flexible and open to change, and more community-focussed than they are now.

However, we recognize that to make this possible, there must be some fundamental changes in the system. Those changes must address our objectives of assuring quality and enhancing opportunity.

And while the principles expressed through the founding statement still seem valid, we believe the system needs a formal mandate that is explicitly stated, that emphasizes the particular role of the colleges in career education in Ontario, and that sets out the values of the colleges as a system.

The colleges have reached a critical juncture in their development. They must renew themselves for the future, or risk becoming progressively less relevant to the needs of the province and its people. And if they are to accomplish a renewal of the system in the coming decade, they must be in a position of strength and confidence. They must have a clear idea of their role in the educational system and the community, and of the values that inform that role.

Our hope is that the government will take the initiative in articulating and facilitating a renewed mandate for the colleges. The mandate should look to the future but also include the essence of what was contained in the original mandate, expressed explicitly and positively.

The mandate we recommend begins with an expression of the purpose of education in general. It speaks to the potential impact of education to foster human awareness and promote understanding, to contribute to the positive development of society, and to open up a world of opportunities for the individual.

 **Recommendation 1**

The Government of Ontario and the Colleges of Applied Arts and Technology should adopt the following mandate for Ontario's colleges:

The Mandate

Preamble

Education has an essential role to play in the development of a world which is peaceful, environmentally sound, equitable and economically viable. Education should help to balance individual and community needs, and foster personal initiative and co-operation within human relationships based on mutual respect.

Education should give people the opportunity to develop the skills and knowledge they need to adapt to and make a constructive contribution to the world in which they live. Education should enhance students' choices and opportunities, and promote the development of individual potential. It should also assist learners in developing their commitment to social responsibility and care for the communities in which they live, and respect for cultural integrity and self-determination of those whose language and traditions may be different from their own.

It is the mandate of the Colleges of Applied Arts and Technology of Ontario:

To provide high-quality career education that enhances students' ability to acquire information, reason clearly, think critically, communicate effectively, apply their knowledge and participate in society as informed and productive citizens.

To make a college education as accessible as possible. Accessibility should include the opportunity to succeed, as well as the opportunity to enrol, and it must be provided in a way that achieves educational equity.

To be responsible, as a system, for quality assurance through system-wide standards and program review.

To work together and with other educational institutions to offer students opportunities for educational mobility and lifelong learning.

To create a dynamic, learner-driven system by anticipating and accommodating the diverse needs of students, both full-time and part-time, enrolled in credit and non-credit courses.

To forge partnerships in and with their communities, including employers, labour, community groups and governments.

To be participatory institutions in which decision-making involves both internal and external stakeholders.

To be model employers in the manner in which they invest in and manage human resource development, in their commitment to equity and in the creation of a positive, healthy and supportive working environment.

The following provides a brief commentary on each section of the mandate.

To provide high-quality career education which enhances students' ability to acquire information, reason clearly, think critically, communicate effectively, apply their knowledge and participate in society as informed and productive citizens.

Colleges must provide learners with career education that will assist their individual development and enhance their employability. Whatever occupational skills with which they graduate, students of the college system must have a strong foundation in generic skills — such as analysis and problem-solving, interpersonal and communications skills — which will help them to adapt to change and make a contribution to the economic and social development of Ontario. In addition to technological literacy, students must be educated in the major issues facing our world. General knowledge, which contributes to self-confident citizenship, and generic skills which are portable and will stand students in good stead for the rest of their lives, must be a significant part of all programs which receive a college credential.

To make a college education as accessible as possible. Accessibility should include the opportunity to succeed, as well as the opportunity to enrol, and it must be provided in a way that achieves educational equity.

The colleges were founded on the ideals of equality of opportunity and the fullest development of each individual's potential. Those ideals must remain touchstones for the college system of the future. The colleges were created to serve secondary school graduates who were not headed for university, out-of-school youth and adults. The colleges of the 1990s and beyond should strive to increase participation by all these groups. They should also be reaching out to those who have traditionally not had access to education beyond high school.

Educational equity involves the identification and removal of systemic barriers to educational opportunities that discriminate against women, visible minorities, aboriginal peoples, persons with disabilities, people living in poverty and members of other groups which have been identified as being underserved with respect to their needs for post-secondary education. Educational equity also involves the implementation of special measures and the application of the concept of reasonable accommodation when these are necessary to achieve and maintain a student group which is representative of the communities served.

Access with success means that all students should have a reasonable chance to achieve in an appropriate college program. This does not guarantee that all students will succeed in their college programs, nor does it remove the individual's responsibility to learn. What it says is that every student should have a fair chance to enrol and succeed, without being encumbered by factors unrelated to his or her ability to benefit from a college education.

To be responsible, as a system, for quality assurance through system-wide standards and program review.

At the same time as colleges encourage accessibility to their programs, they must ensure that students receive a quality education. There should be system-wide outcome standards and review for all programs which grant a college credential. That way, both students and society have the assurance that college graduates have certain knowledge and skills, according to the diploma or certificate they have received.

To work together and with other educational institutions to offer students opportunities for educational mobility and lifelong learning.

The educational system in Ontario needs to break down some of the barriers between and within the different types of institutions in order to improve the ability of students to move through the system. Students should be able to earn portable credits which can be applied to another program in another college. There should be assessment of prior learning and experience for those who come to college after some time in the workforce or from other educational jurisdictions. Links with the school system should improve the transition for students from secondary school to college; and links with universities should improve student opportunities for advanced training.

The concept of lifelong learning is becoming a watchword in the educational community. It refers to creating a learning environment which does not simply tolerate the recurrent student, but welcomes and nurtures this learner by recognizing his or her particular needs and by being flexible and adaptable enough to meet them.

To create a dynamic, learner-driven system by anticipating and accommodating the diverse needs of students, both full-time and part-time, enrolled in credit and non-credit courses.

In a learner-driven system, administrative and institutional structures must be shaped by student needs. Colleges should provide students with "passports" of learning, enabling them to earn "stamps" of credit in places and in ways which suit their individual needs. Adult learners should be able to take college programs on a flexible timetable and in off-campus locations which allow them to meet their continuing work and family responsibilities. Colleges should respond to the needs not only of students seeking credit courses toward a credential, but those seeking personal-interest, non-credit courses to make their lives more interesting and fulfilling.

To forge partnerships in and with their communities, including employers, labour, community groups and governments.

Colleges have always been community-focussed institutions. However, the communities they serve are becoming increasingly diverse and so are the needs of those communities. To serve them well, colleges must engage in outreach activities and must form partnerships with a range of constituencies. Partnerships with business and industry, labour, government, public agencies and a range of community organizations will help to ensure that college programs and services are relevant and up to date, as well as help to identify emerging needs.

To be participatory institutions in which decision-making involves both internal and external stakeholders.

Stakeholders, both internal and external to the colleges, should be part of the decision-making structure. Collaboration in college governance is necessary for keeping the colleges in touch with their communities. It is also essential that those who work and learn in the colleges participate in the decision-making process. Without this type of reciprocal commitment, it will be impossible for colleges to keep up with changing student needs.

To be model employers in the manner in which they invest in and manage human resource development, in their commitment to equity and in the creation of a positive, healthy and supportive working environment.

Institutions dedicated to education and training must invest in the development of their own human resources. They must also practice the equity they preach. The colleges can influence their students and their communities by practicing exemplary employer behaviour.

3.4 Fulfilling the Mandate

We have stated that this renewed mandate is not achievable, in our view, without fundamental change in the system. We are also aware that it is important to set priorities for change.

The dual focus of this report, on the objectives of assuring quality and enhancing access, reflects the priorities of the many important stakeholders we consulted.

The chapters which follow discuss these priorities and how we believe they should be addressed. Recommendations are directed at government, the system and individual colleges. While different constituencies may disagree on which issues should be acted on first or foremost, there is broad support for the view that we have identified the critical pressure points for change. (A complete list of recommendations is found in Appendix E.)

Chapter 4 tackles the issues surrounding the quality of college credential programs. The chapter addresses the characteristics and processes pertaining to the generic skills and general education content of programs, system-wide standards and program review.

Chapter 5 examines the opportunity to participate in college education. The focus of this chapter is on serving the diversity of needs in communities, including issues of equity, assisting the underprepared student, and providing programs in adult basic education.

Chapter 6 looks at ways to improve both quality and opportunity by proposing ways to strengthen the links across the educational spectrum through a system for prior learning assessment, a provincial body for co-ordinating school-college links and an institute to facilitate opportunities for advanced training.

Chapter 7 discusses initiatives aimed at facilitating the realization of quality and opportunity through more system-wide strategic planning, greater sharing of specialized resources within the college system, and more stable and co-ordinated government funding.

Chapter 8 deals with one of the most central elements of any strategy for improving quality and opportunity: human resource development in the college system.

Chapter 9 summarizes the ways in which the renewed mandate proposed by Vision 2000 calls for new initiatives by local college boards and the Ontario Council of Regents.

Chapter 10 indicates where Vision 2000 sees the starting points for change along the road to renewal.

4

Partners in Quality

4.1 Preamble

The mission of the colleges begins with the obligation to provide high-quality career-oriented education which enhances students' ability to acquire information, reason clearly, think critically, communicate effectively, apply their knowledge, and participate in society as informed and productive citizens. Providing learners with career education that will assist their individual development and enhance their employability must be, in our view, the cornerstone of the colleges' role.

Providing the specific skills necessary to do a job — whether it is soil mechanics, computer-assisted design, or sports administration — will always be an important part of what the colleges do. But it is also essential that the students who graduate from a college of applied arts and technology have the general knowledge and skills that will allow them to continue learning, both on and off the job, throughout their lives. There are widespread concerns — which we share — that the colleges are providing career education that is too narrowly focussed on specific job skills.

Vision 2000 believes that significant changes must be made to broaden the education students receive by reorienting college programs to put more emphasis on general education and what we have called generic skills.

We also believe that the college system must accept responsibility for assuring the quality and consistency of a college credential. We agree with the many stakeholders who emphasize the need for system-wide standards and program review to provide "a common hallmark of academic quality"[9] for graduates of college programs.

---

[9] Michael Park, "Expanding the Core: General Education, Generic Skills , and Core Curriculum in Ontario Community Colleges," in *Challenges to the College and the College System. Background Papers* (Toronto: Ontario Council of Regents, 1990), p. 1.

Reorienting the curriculum to provide more general education and generic skills, and introducing system-wide standards and program review, will, in our view, serve to enhance quality and increase respect for a college credential. Social and economic returns will accrue both to the individual and to society as a whole. Colleges are public institutions, and, as such, their responsibility is to serve both individual learners and the community at large. We believe the recommendations which follow in this chapter will enhance the value of a college education for those who obtain it, and will increase confidence in the abilities of college graduates among employers and others. These recommendations are also intended to ensure that college graduates will be better able to make a contribution to the economic and social development of Ontario.

What is at stake, we believe, is the credibility of the college system.

4.2 Definition of Terms

This section defines the programs we are focussing on and the terms we are using.

College credential programs: First, our focus in this chapter is on those programs for which a college post-secondary credential is granted. Since there are a wide variety of programs and credentials offered in the colleges, these terms deserve some explanation.

Credential programs are defined, for the purposes of this report, as career-oriented programs for which the colleges determine both entry and exit requirements. These include the programs that have traditionally been termed post-secondary diploma and certificate programs. The defining features of these programs are: entry requirements of Grade 12 or equivalent; one, two or three years of full-time equivalent study, including post-diploma studies, traditionally in the broad areas of health, business, technology, and applied arts; admission, curriculum and graduation requirements determined by the colleges in conjunction with the Ministry of Colleges and Universities (MCU); and formula funding provided through MCU.

Non-credential activities: These can be defined as those career-oriented programs over which the colleges do not control entry and exit standards and those programs and courses which are not primarily vocational in nature. The latter includes general-interest courses which help meet important individual and community needs and often provide an introduction to other educational opportunities at the colleges.

Non-credential career-oriented activities are crucial to the colleges' role in provincial skills development. Such activities differ from the credential programs, which have been defined here strictly in terms of one-, two- and three-year programs fully controlled by the college, in a number of important respects. First, non-credential activities have traditionally addressed more immediate (often short-term), narrowly defined and readily identifiable needs: for example, specific skills training, such as employer-sponsored training for upgrading to a new machine used in a plant's production process; or basic academic upgrading, such as literacy or numeracy training to meet the needs of target groups without a secondary school diploma.

Second, access to these non-credential activities has been limited to, or targeted at, a particular group, and admission has not been under the control of the colleges. Examples of these activities are courses targeted at unemployed youth, women in non-traditional trades, or employees of a particular firm. Third, curriculum content and delivery frequently have been designed to the specifications or subject to the approval of the sponsoring party. Fourth, funding has been provided by a variety of sources, including Canada Employment and Immigration, the Ministry of Skills Development, individual employers, unions and community groups.

We believe it is important for bridges to be built between the non-credential activities and credential programs in the colleges, and we propose some links in subsequent chapters of this report. For example, in Chapter 6, we make recommendations related to granting credit for prior learning and experience, which might be attained through college activities that are in the non-credential area. We expect that a new emphasis on general education and generic skills in the college credential programs will encourage sponsors of non-credential programs to set similar standards.

Our focus in this chapter on the credential programs is not intended to relegate other college activities to lesser importance. Rather, we believe that efforts to enhance quality in the colleges will be most productive by focussing on activities over which the college community, broadly defined, exercises explicit control.

General education and generic skills: In the context of the colleges, we define general education to be: "the broad study of subjects and issues which are central to education for life in our culture. Centred in, but not restricted to, the arts, sciences, literature and humanities, general education encourages students to know and understand themselves, their society and institutions, and their roles and responsibilities as citizens."[10]

We define generic skills to be: "practical life skills essential for both personal and career success. They include language and communications skills, math skills, learning and thinking skills, interpersonal skills, and basic technological literacy. They are not job-specific, but are crucial to mastering changing technologies, changing environments and changing jobs ... Facility in some generic skills — reading, listening, writing, learning — is a prerequisite for success in most college-level courses."[11]

Generic skills may be taught in discrete courses, such as communications or mathematics, but they may also be integrated across the curriculum. Improving learning, thinking and communication skills need not be confined to a single course. While general education tends to be more subject-oriented and contained in particular courses, such as history or English literature, or organized into a human studies program, it too can be reinforced in the teaching of vocational subjects.

---

10 Park, op. cit., p. 2.

11 Park, op. cit., p. 2.

4.3 Reorienting the Curriculum

Vision 2000 believes that the provision of general education and generic skills should be significantly increased in programs which receive a college credential.

We referred in Chapter 2 to the concerns raised by both internal and external stakeholders that the college curriculum is overly concentrated on specific skills training, to the detriment, and sometimes to the exclusion, of general education. There is a perception among many people within the colleges, as well as outside, that college career-oriented education must go beyond narrow job-related skills to enable students to realize their personal and career goals.

The debate about how broad a college education should be is not a new one. However, it has been lent more urgency by the rapidly changing economic environment, which demands a labour force which can adapt to new technologies and learn new skills. The need for a refrigeration technologist to understand refrigeration is obvious. However, it is also essential for that technologist to be able to write a clear and concise report, and to communicate and work effectively with customers and co-workers. As new technologies change the processes of production and the organization of production and relationships within an enterprise, the ability of the technologist to acquire new skills will be crucial to the future of both the worker and the enterprise.

In the current environment, a worker who lacks appropriate language and communication skills or basic technological literacy is at a distinct disadvantage. In today's fast-changing marketplace, workers require a portable and expandable skills base. Such a base gives them greater security of employment by enabling them to adapt to changing job demands by updating or upgrading skills and to shift between jobs with different skill requirements.

Increasingly, employers are asking that college graduates have the ability to learn additional skills, to work with others, to solve problems and to communicate clearly. These skills are becoming more valued because both the speed and nature of economic change make adaptability a requirement. From the perspective of employers, a focus on generic skills assists them to use both capital and human resources more flexibly in adjusting to the impact of technological change and competitive pressures. While specific skills training may be firm or job-specific, a focus on generic skills as a foundation of the college curriculum would benefit employers as a whole.

In addition, the communications revolution has expanded the horizons of citizenship so that people can and should feel part of local, national and international debates on issues that affect them, their families and their futures — issues such as poverty, the environment, the Canadian constitution or political change in other parts of the world. To participate actively, they should be aware of the background and context of current events and issues. Helping people to be good citizens, as well as productive workers with marketable skills, should be part of the educational experience at a college.

The need to broaden or enrich college career-oriented education is reinforced at this time by the convergence of opinion among many stakeholders, both within and outside the college system. During the Vision 2000 consultation process, representatives of employers and labour supported a broadening of the curriculum to include more general education and generic skills, as did community groups, college faculty and administrators and others.

> Employers, workers, students and teachers have all told Vision 2000 that too many among the current crop of Ontario community college graduates are deficient in generic skills and general education, to the detriment of our graduates' career success and the future performance of the Ontario economy.[12]

A growing body of research is also supportive of this direction.

> Technological knowledge and capabilities are diffused not through the sale of products or blueprints in international markets, but through national or regional communities which share a certain base of knowledge and the increments to that knowledge ... The role of the college system in transmitting the fundamental skills needed by a diverse array of learners will be critical in providing the skills and knowledge base essential for this innovative process.[13]

For many stakeholders, the question is not whether the curriculum should be changed, but how best to do it. They note that the existing provincial guideline of 30 per cent general education content is, in most cases, not being met. They ask what can be done differently that will achieve the goal of a more well-rounded curriculum.[14]

Convinced of the need for a *significantly* greater emphasis on general education and generic skills, Vision 2000 had to wrestle with how to achieve this objective. As we have noted, there are guidelines that indicate general education should constitute at least 30 per cent of the content of post-secondary programs. But many programs have considerably less. We considered recommending that general education and generic skills should constitute 50 per cent of program content. However, specifying a fixed proportion of each program's content or courses would not necessarily achieve the outcomes we desire.

Traditionally, an orientation to time or percentage of courses has meant adding and subtracting program hours or courses in a program. We do not wish to use this as the basis for our approach to the development of curriculum and delivery required to achieve more general education and generic skills. Current programs differ widely, both within and between colleges, in their general education

---

[12] Park, op. cit., p. 5.

[13] David Wolfe, "New Technology and Education: A Challenge for the Colleges," in *Colleges and the Changing Economy. Background Papers* (Toronto: Ontario Council of Regents, 1989), p. 16.

[14] It has been noted that the erosion in the teaching of general education and generic skills has been due, at least in part, to funding pressures. See Norman Rowen, *Pressures for Change, Opportunities for Development* (Toronto: Ontario Council of Regents, 1989), pp. 7-8; and Instructional Assignment Review Committee, *Survival or Excellence?* (Toronto: Ministry of Colleges and Universities, 1985), p. 93. Such pressures have contributed to reductions in program hours and considerable differences in generic and general education content in programs sharing the same objectives.

requirements; we believe this is a result of an emphasis on counting hours and courses of instruction, rather than measuring educational attainments and outcomes.

After considerable debate, we concluded that the objectives we share are best achieved by recommending a significant increase in the general education and generic skills content of college programs to achieve an equivalence of learning outcomes. The absence of a fixed percentage should not be interpreted as suggesting that only minimal change is required. On the contrary, the recommendation should be taken as literally as necessary to produce a curriculum with significant increases in general education and generic skills. We are advocating nothing less than a major reorientation of the curriculum in the direction of general education and generic skills.

 Recommendation 2

> **There should be a significant increase in the generic skills and general education content of programs leading to a college credential to ensure an equivalence of learning outcomes between these components and specific occupational skills.**

In undertaking this direction, it should be possible to integrate much of the increased generic skills content into courses which currently focus on specific vocational skills. We envision, for example, that generic communications skills training would be embodied in career-oriented courses across the curriculum, as well as in some specifically designated communications courses.

It is possible that some of the increased general education content of programs may be integrated into occupation-specific courses. However, it is likely that additional discrete offerings will also be required. For example, a student of engineering technology might learn about the importance to the environment of reducing industrial emissions in an occupation-specific course, but might gain a broader perspective on the environment in a separate course on global environmental conditions.

Placing greater emphasis on generic skills and general education will not necessarily lead to a lengthening of college programs. Consultations with employers revealed that their willingness and ability to undertake a greater role in providing job-specific training would be enhanced if their employees possessed well-developed basic skills. We frequently heard statements such as: "The colleges should give the basic education, and we'll train on the job" and "There is a powerful role for the colleges in our sector. Don't teach how to operate XYZ machine; teach them the fundamentals in writing, math, and science; and teach them to learn; and prepare them to have to learn and learn again throughout their lifetimes."[15]

While we do not propose that the colleges diminish the job-specific content of their programs to the extent that might be implied in the preceding statements, it should be possible to revise college curriculum in the directions we have recommended without significantly altering the length of programs. Some judicious reductions in the narrowest specific skills components of existing college programs should be possible without diminishing the overall vocational orientation of college

[15] Audrey Gill, "Role of the Colleges in the Changing Economy: Report on Consultations," in *Colleges and the Changing Economy. Background Papers* (Toronto: Ontario Council of Regents, 1989), pp. 11, 15.

programs. This possibility depends, however, on employers translating their words into action, through taking greater responsibility for job-specific training.

It may also require some reorientation in how students view a college education. Many current college students are attracted to the colleges because programs are perceived as providing training which enables them to immediately perform on the job at a high level. The colleges and the secondary schools will need to demonstrate to students the necessity of embarking on a lifelong learning process and the importance of solid foundation skills to this process. Students will need to be convinced, for example, that the acquisition of these foundation skills will make it easier and faster to acquire specific skills both in an adult educational setting and on the job. Similarly, employers' hiring practices for entry-level jobs will need to be consistent with this thinking and reinforce it.

In short, the success and the costs of educational reform at the college level depend, to a large measure, on complementary actions being undertaken by both secondary schools and employers.

We believe that the explicit and expanded inclusion of generic skills and general education in all programs leading to a college credential is central to the future development of the colleges and their communities. The challenge of equipping learners with the knowledge, skills and abilities needed for Ontario's evolving economy requires that we acknowledge the considerable uncertainty about which specific skills will be needed. We must concentrate on constructing the foundations upon which further skills can be built and from which society will realize the greatest social return.

The focus on general education and generic skills will involve a fundamental reorientation of college curricula. To achieve our goals will require that college educators, both faculty, staff and administrators, undertake a major process of renewal of curriculum and delivery methods at each college. The process will need to be guided by the establishment, on a system-wide basis, of clear learning outcomes for each program leading to a college credential. In providing for such outcomes, we envision considerable diversity across the system in the organization and delivery of general education, generic skills and job-specific skills.

The development of system-wide standards for learning outcomes is discussed in the next section of this chapter, followed by our recommendation for ongoing, system-wide program review in the subsequent section. Finally, a mechanism to guide these changes in direction is the subject of Section 4.6. The important implications of these changes for human resource and curriculum development are discussed in Chapter 8.

4.4 System-Wide Standards

Vision 2000 sees a clear need for system-wide standards as a basis for monitoring and improving educational quality in college programs. These standards should focus on learning outcomes expected of graduates of college credential programs, including outcomes relating to general education and generic skills.

Establishing system-wide program standards represents a fundamental shift for the colleges. There is a broad consensus among stakeholders that standards which apply to graduates at all colleges are necessary, and that this change need not unduly restrict institutional autonomy. System-wide standards will ensure the equivalence of programs across the province. No group with whom we consulted, either within or outside the colleges, suggested that colleges should be differentiated with respect to quality.

Currently, in the absence of program standards which apply to every college, there is understandable confusion about the meaning and value of college credentials. Employers have told Vision 2000 that they see a "widely fluctuating range of skills and knowledge in graduates from college to college, from program to program, even from teacher to teacher ..."[16] They argue that the words "college graduate" do not seem to have a common meaning across the system.

The college system must be able to assure learners, employers and the public that the programs provided by the colleges are of consistently high quality and that they are current and relevant to the needs of the community. System-wide standards are needed to ensure that graduates of a given program, from any college, have achieved a clearly defined level of knowledge, skill and ability in their field.

Credentials are the common currency of education. College credentials must reflect the value of the activities and attainments of the colleges and their graduates. Prospective students and employers, in particular, should have a clear understanding of what a credential from a college program implies in terms of student attainment. Variations in standards between colleges make it difficult for college credentials to convey the appropriate information about the attainments of learners. Each credential should be defined to clearly denote significant differences among programs in the nature and level of curricula. Just as each subsequent credential should reflect increasingly complex occupational knowledge and skills, so should each reflect important increments in the general education and generic skills that students have learned.

An additional problem is the use of particular titles for credentials. College "certificates" are now granted for both short-term, pre-diploma programs and some post-diploma programs, while "diplomas" are granted for two- and three-year programs. Titles should clearly reflect distinctions in the level and nature of curriculum.

Employers are not alone in expressing concern. Vision 2000 heard support from a variety of stakeholders, within and outside the college community, for consistent course and program requirements, including exit requirements, that would be recognized and supported by the colleges, employers, government and other stakeholders, including professional associations and licensing bodies.

Common definitions for programs and for what constitutes a credit are seen as particularly important if students are to have mobility between programs, between colleges, and between colleges

---

16 Park, op. cit., p. 1

and other educational institutions. Access for many future learners is expected to depend upon the flexibility to "stop out"; that is, to acquire credits toward a credential over a period of time, on a full-time or part-time basis, and perhaps in more than one institution. Consistent program standards will facilitate this kind of recurrent learning.

Consultations conducted independently by MCU provide substantiation — from both college and industry sources — for the view that consistent standards are necessary and desirable.[17] MCU's review of program standards also indicates the usefulness of provincial standards in providing a focus for updating programs to keep them relevant, particularly in fields subject to rapid change, such as technology.

In addition, the recent report on accessibility prepared by the Ontario Council on University Affairs noted the perception that "standards in CAAT programs need to be reviewed, and ways need to be found to ensure a more uniform standard across the system for similar programs."[18]

There have been some efforts within the system to address the need for system-wide standards. For example, the Heads of Technology in the colleges have been working together to develop system-wide learning outcomes for technology programs. Vision 2000 believes there are major benefits to be gained by developing standards for all programs that lead to a college credential.

It is important to note that our goal is consistency in program *outcomes*, not standardization of delivery. Standards should provide colleges with a description of the outcomes of the learning process. But local colleges must retain their autonomy in determining how programs will be delivered to meet these standards. The need to ensure sufficient flexibility to deliver programs in a manner most suitable to local needs figures prominently in consultations on program standards.

Because we are focussing on learning attainments, factors such as the length of programs, full-time or part-time status, location of the learning (on campus or job site, for example), and mode of learning (in-class, self-directed, co-op, distance education, etc.) are not relevant to the setting of standards. We believe that uniformity in delivery or specific content should not be a result of defining standards. Colleges' ability to be flexible and responsive depends on this distinction. Vision 2000 views system-wide standards for program outcomes and local diversity in program delivery as complementary. Our objective is to ensure the quality and consistency of what is learned, not to standardize how it is learned.

In order for the benefits of system-wide standards to be realized, it will be important to:

- provide for the necessary balance of generic skills and general education content with specific skills training;
- establish mechanisms for regular, system-wide program reviews for the purposes of maintaining appropriate standards and evaluating how well standards are being met;

---

[17] Ontario Ministry of Colleges and Universities, *Provincial Program Standards* (Toronto: MCU, April 1989).

[18] Ontario Council on University Affairs, *What The Council Heard About Accessibility: The Ontario Dilemma* (Toronto: OCUA, 1990), p. 22.

- provide for the explicit involvement of the broad range of stakeholders, both internal and external to the colleges, in the development and implementation of system-wide standards;

- ensure that learners have access to the "front-end" services of assessment and preparatory activities that will provide a reasonable probability of success in their programs; and

- provide for major initiatives in curriculum and professional development, as well as the development of alternative delivery forms.

In sum, the system must develop good standards — standards which are current and relevant, include clearly identified outcomes for all areas, and provide for local determination of specific content and delivery. We believe these will most likely emerge not from a single group or constituency, be it professional association, college constituency or MCU, but rather from the co-operation and active involvement of all relevant stakeholders. We believe that a process in which standards were determined by any single group would prove ineffective and lack the credibility and commitment that the system requires.

 Recommendation 3

There should be system-wide standards for all programs leading to a college credential. Such standards must focus on the learning outcomes expected of graduates from a program.

4.5 Program Review

"Quality does not happen by chance, but is a result of continuous efforts directed toward maintaining and enhancing it."[19]

Vision 2000 believes it is essential to have regular system-wide program review in order to ensure that system-wide standards are maintained and that programs that lead to a college credential are meeting the learning outcomes required by those standards.

Regular review of programs is among the principal means whereby the system can exercise a quality assurance function. It has been noted that quality is a relative concept. "Thus, an appropriate assessment of quality consists of two parts — setting or acknowledging a standard and determining how various aspects of a program measure up to that standard."[20]

Program review should be linked specifically to the accreditation of programs. Accreditation is the process of evaluation of a program or course which determines whether it meets the standards

---

[19] Instructional Assignment Review Committee, *Survival or Excellence?* (Toronto: Ministry of Colleges and Universities, July 1985), p. 90.

[20] Melvin D. George, "Assessing Program Quality," in *Designing Academic Program Reviews* (R. F. Wilson, editor), New Directions for Higher Education, No. 37 (San Francisco: Jossey-Bass, 1982) p. 49.

necessary for a credential to be granted. Currently, most college programs go through an approval process by MCU prior to being offered by the college. However, once the program is approved, there is no regular review by the Ministry. Some selected programs, mainly in the health sciences, are accredited on an ongoing basis by agencies external to the colleges.

Currently, individual colleges have the responsibility for assuring quality for the vast majority of their programs. The operational review process, initiated by MCU, is one means by which colleges are required to assess their own program review processes. However, the nature and extent of individual college program review have varied greatly, and there is no system-wide review function in place for the majority of programs.

A study for MCU of accreditation options in 1978 noted that "the internal evaluation process in the individual colleges is weak and somewhat inconsistent,"[21] and the evidence provided by our research and consultations suggests that this conclusion remains true. The report notes the lack of agreement on "appropriate [system-wide] terminal objectives" or system consensus on models for evaluation, a view confirmed in both the discussion paper *Provincial Program Standards*[22] and the *Report of the Accreditation Review Committee*.[23]

In 1985, the Instructional Assignment Review Committee (IARC) observed that "there appears to be little in the way of systematic review of program quality in the colleges — beyond examination of statistics on placement and attrition rates — except in the limited number of programs which are subject to compulsory certification by professional bodies."[24] The IARC noted that unless there is an ongoing commitment to monitoring quality, there is no way of assessing the level of quality or whether it is improving or declining.

For Vision 2000, the major issue is not whether an individual college undertakes a selective review of particular programs, although we believe internal assessment is essential. Rather, we want to ensure that there is a commitment to regular, system-wide program review, and that the review process is directed by a representative system-wide body.

We realize that the principle of establishing system-wide program review is not new to the colleges; both the 1978 MCU study and the 1985 IARC report suggested it, without apparent success. We recommend it here in the expectation that the weight of evidence and opinion will now carry it forward. While there may be debate as to how the review process should be carried out, or who should do it, support for the function is substantial and widespread.

Regular system-wide program review is essential to assuring the effectiveness of our recommendations on system-wide standards and general education and generic skills. The process of

---

[21] Ted Zaharchuk and Jane Palmer, *A Report on Accreditation in the Colleges of Applied Arts and Technology* (Toronto: Decision Dynamics Corporation, 1978), p. 69.

[22] Ministry of Colleges and Universities, April 1989.

[23] Ministry of Colleges and Universities, June 1989.

[24] Instructional Assignment Review Committee, op. cit., p. 125.

system-wide program review that we envisage will provide an appropriate means for assuring consistency in the quality of all college credential programs.

 Recommendation 4

All programs leading to a college credential should be subject to regular, system-wide program review for the purposes of accreditation.

In this next section, we recommend the establishment of a representative body to guide the standards and review process of the college system. However, it is important to clarify at this point that this body would have overall responsibility for program review of all programs across the system that lead to a college credential. It would also have explicit representation from a variety of internal and external stakeholders.

This system-wide body would develop the framework for program reviews. It would establish consistent, system-wide guidelines which would be program-specific and would focus on indicators appropriate to the evaluation of program outcomes. The guidelines would outline the process to be used in the review. Programs in a given program area would be evaluated concurrently across the system. Those conducting the reviews would be experts in the field and, for the most part, external to the colleges, including, where appropriate, experts from other jurisdictions.

The guidelines would not provide a fully comprehensive array of indicators, but rather would establish a core set of measures capable of providing information crucial to the evaluation of program outcomes. These measures would be applied at each college in order to permit system-wide comparison. Colleges, however, would be able to utilize additional measures to provide data relevant to their particular concerns.

It is important to consider program review and accreditation as an ongoing process, rather than one only associated with the initial approval of programs, a function which we suggest should remain with MCU. The focus for program review and continued accreditation should be to assure that the outcomes defined for the program are appropriate (i.e. current and relevant); and to determine the extent to which these outcomes are being achieved.

The approach to program review we envisage emphasizes the goal-based model which focuses on learning outcomes, as well as the responsive model which provides for diverse stakeholders to articulate and reconcile their different views of quality. We believe this approach is appropriate for the colleges, with their great variety of stakeholder interests and perspectives. It also incorporates elements of the "connoisseurship" model, which relies on the judgment of a small group of experts and is used by the Ontario university system in its appraisal of graduate programs.[25]

---

[25] A discussion of the various approaches to program review is found in Norman Rowen, "Toward a Self-Governing System: Some Aspects of Quality and Proposals for Change," in *Challenges to the College and the College System. Background Papers* (Toronto: Ontario Council of Regents, 1990). The distinction between the responsive and connoisseurship models of program evaluation, and the application of the latter in the Ontario university system are discussed in Michael Skolnik, "How Academic Program Review Can Foster Intellectual Conformity and Stifle Diversity of Thought and Method," *Journal of Higher Education* (Ohio State University Press, 1988), Vol. 60, No. 6.

Regular program review has several implications for the colleges. First, program objectives would be revised on an ongoing basis in light of information systematically collected from all colleges offering a particular program.

Second, collecting and analyzing comparable information from across the system will allow for discussion of the efficiency and effectiveness of alternative delivery modes in a given program area. This would assist local colleges in determining their approaches to content and delivery. The benefits of different instructional approaches would be shared among the colleges.

Third, the results of program review would provide the basis for initiatives in staff, faculty and curriculum development, and the upgrading of equipment required to meet accepted standards.

Fourth, where lack of student demand resulted in the inability of a college to provide a critical mass of faculty and equipment necessary to meet the standards, the benefits of continuing the program could be more rigourously assessed.

Fifth, the results of such reviews would, in extreme cases, lead to programs having their accreditation removed, with the associated loss in funding.

Finally, this focus would provide an impetus for the development of a variety of evaluation measures and instruments, including new means to assess learners, to gain the input of employers and graduates about required competencies and program outcomes, and measures to explicitly examine instructional processes.

To accommodate program differences, the system-wide body would establish guidelines for program reviews, which would likely vary in specificity depending on the nature and needs of the program. It would be the responsibility of the system-wide body to ensure that reviews consider a range of indicators that might show how and how well the objectives of a particular program have been attained and whether changes in the standards themselves are necessary to ensure the relevance of college offerings.

Another important consideration is the need to separate the review and accreditation of programs from the licensing of practitioners. Several practitioner bodies have sought to establish their authority over who will be allowed to practise a particular occupation (e.g. in technology and accountancy). Such attempts at licensing have been allowed in relatively few instances and generally under the rubric of safeguarding the public good. While the need for external licensing may not entirely disappear, we believe that system-wide standards and program review will reduce the number of such instances considerably.

The inclusion of licensing bodies in the proposed accreditation structure and process may help to alleviate difficulties such as those experienced in the physiotherapist and occupational therapist programs. These programs were eventually transferred from the colleges to the universities because the professional associations refused to accredit them. In addition, similar problems involving licensing have arisen with technician and technologist programs involving the Ontario Association of Certified Engineering Technicians and Technologists and the Association of Professional Engineers of

Ontario, and may arise with social service occupations, early childhood education specialists, accountants and others. We believe the government should continue to exercise care in granting licensing authority to individual groups that we expect will now be represented on the new system-wide body overseeing college programs.

4.6 College Standards and Accreditation Council

The colleges, prospective learners, employers and the public require that colleges be accountable for their programs. We propose in this section that a provincial council, broadly based and representative of the various internal and external stakeholders in the system, be given authority for system-wide program standards, review and accreditation.

The rationale for such a structure is clear and direct: the colleges must operate more as a system for the purpose of assuring and enhancing the quality of programs which receive a college credential. The appropriate means to embody such a commitment to quality must include the participation of the college community, broadly defined to include representatives of the academic, support and administrative staff of the colleges, college alumni, labour, community representatives, employers (public and private), professional associations, educators from secondary schools and universities, and governments.

The structure of the College Standards and Accreditation Council (CSAC), which we propose, has been carefully considered by Vision 2000 and has received support from several different sources. For example, following extensive consultations and research, three study teams, each composed of a variety of stakeholders and examining different aspects of the colleges' role, arrived independently at recommendations for this type of representative body.

A similar structure of representation for the purposes of setting standards and reviewing programs has been implemented in other jurisdictions, most recently in New Zealand. The February 1989 report of the New Zealand Ministry of Education, entitled *Learning for Life*, outlines the functions of the National Educational Qualifications Authority. These include setting and reviewing standards, and accrediting programs for the purposes of granting credentials and securing public funding.

Such a structure was proposed for Ontario more than a decade ago in the 1978 accreditation study for MCU. Its introduction will require no less a commitment now than it would have then. The difference, perhaps, is that the demands on the colleges have become greater and more urgent, as the widespread support for such a structure indicates.

The responsibilities of CSAC would include a role as guarantor of overall academic quality and direction, primarily through the setting of standards and program review, representing the system in academic matters, assuring that general education and generic skills components are incorporated and maintained in all programs, and providing overall consistency in the awarding of credentials.

We consider it eminently reasonable and responsible that the same broadly based and representative body responsible for establishing the outcomes of programs should be responsible for evaluating whether and how such outcomes are achieved.

Developing a means to share responsibilities for setting standards and evaluating and accrediting programs will be a crucial but challenging task. We believe it is impractical and ineffective to have individual colleges solely responsible for these activities. This would continue to result in unacceptable differences among colleges and fail to meet the important objective of enhancing the quality of programs system-wide.

Alternatively, having quality determined by a body external to the colleges (be it a ministry, professional association or other body) would, we believe, be far less effective than our proposal. The approach we offer would provide a means by which the college system can assume not only ownership of quality, but also exercise this responsibility in partnership with external stakeholders. In addition, an approach emphasizing external control would run counter to the values and culture of the colleges and would likely meet with considerable resistance.

 Recommendation 5

A College Standards and Accreditation Council (CSAC) should be established, with participation of internal and external stakeholders and with executive authority in the areas of system-wide program standards, review and accreditation.

Members of CSAC would be appointed by the Council of Regents (COR). Half the members would be nominated by constituencies internal to the colleges, including administrators, faculty, and staff. The other half would be drawn from government and external constituencies, including small and large employers, labour, and professional associations. The Chair would be appointed by order-in-council.

The members could be appointed for time-limited but renewable terms, perhaps for three years, on an overlapping basis to provide for continuity. When members have been carefully selected and are representative, this body will have the stature and professional competence required to enhance the system as a whole, without limiting local initiative in how college programs are delivered.

It is recommended that CSAC become independently associated with the COR for organizational purposes, and retain its independence in a manner similar to the academic council of the Ontario Council on University Affairs; that is, COR could comment on, but not alter, CSAC decisions.

In addition, we suggest that CSAC create a series of program councils which would have important practical responsibilities. These would include:

- Developing standards for different program areas. This includes setting entrance criteria, program objectives and standards of achievement (learning outcomes) to be required for each level of certification.

- Developing criteria and procedures for the regular review of all programs under their auspices. The needs of particular programs might require unique approaches to program evaluation. While program reviews would focus on evaluating learning outcomes, there will be cases where the program councils examine the instructional process and resources affecting the attainment of program outcomes.

- Developing a sectoral planning capability. The determination of industry requirements and possible student interest will be important in planning new programs to meet emerging needs. Such sectoral planning should be carried out in conjunction with other bodies which might be developed as a result of recommendations by the Premier's Council on Technology.

Program councils will need sufficient lead time to establish program outcomes. Colleges will need time to revise curriculum and provide professional development for faculty. Given the composition of the program councils, they will be well situated to initiate the collection of sector-specific information and co-ordinate program development.

The program councils might be established around a cluster of programs in areas such as information and administration (formerly business), manufacturing and skilled trades (formerly technology), health and healing, social and developmental services, creative and applied arts, environment and natural resources, and hospitality and tourism.

Each program council would be composed of members with relevant professional experience and, like CSAC, would include representation from the college system and from appropriate external groups. These councils would be representative of a broader range of stakeholders than, for example, the currently constituted operating committees (e.g. Heads of Business) of the Association of Colleges of Applied Arts and Technology of Ontario.

Roles of college boards of governors: CSAC would not significantly alter the roles of college boards. The boards would continue to be responsible for the overall well-being of their colleges, with some clarified responsibilities.

Boards would have to demonstrate that programs meet provincial standards. This would be accomplished through their participation in program reviews conducted under the auspices of CSAC. Where reviews indicated areas needing improvement, boards would be responsible for developing and implementing remedial action.

Boards, however, would continue to determine the mix of offerings that best meet local needs — both credential and non-credential programs, including fee-for-service activity. They would be relatively unencumbered[26] in providing contract training to local employers and governments, with the proviso that such programs would not, in themselves, offer a college credential. However, individuals would be able to gain credit toward a credential to the extent that the training included outcomes required for a credential. The planning and development of new programs would rest largely with individual colleges, and boards would decide the specific content and delivery form of credential programs. In addition, boards would be responsible for the ongoing updating of resources — capital, human and curricular.

------

26 Subject to financial and accountability guidelines as developed under Recommendation 14 (see Chapter 5).

Boards would continue seeking advice from local program advisory committees, college councils, administration, faculty, staff, community groups, etc. There is little reason for CSAC to intrude in how a college board exercises its responsibilities.

Role of local program advisory committees: The role of existing local program advisory committees, composed of employers, college graduates and people working in a program-related occupation, would remain important. With the directions we envision, new program initiatives would continue to require the leadership and support of these committees. Advisory committees would continue to play a key role in advising on curriculum and delivery issues. As well, we assume local boards would want to include their participation in aspects of program review, under CSAC. Some colleges have organized their program advisory committees around clusters of related programs. We expect that other colleges might choose to do the same so that their local advisory groups would correspond to CSAC program councils.

Role of the Ministry: In two major academic areas, MCU would continue to have primary responsibility: first, for allocation of funds to accredited programs and, second, for final approval of new program proposals. Through CSAC, program councils would forward their proposals for new programs that are not currently offered in the colleges but which respond to identified needs. Proposals from individual colleges for new programs in existing areas would be sent through CSAC to the Ministry, with the advice of the relevant program council.

The Ministry's responsibility for program approval must be understood as distinct from CSAC's responsibility for program review and accreditation. As noted above, the Ministry has confined its activities in this area to initial program approval. This function serves purposes other than quality assessment (e.g. determination of need); and, to the extent that quality is a consideration, the Ministry can reasonably assess only the proposed program content and delivery. CSAC's responsibility for ongoing program review can thus be seen as a necessary complement to the Ministry's role in initial program approval.

Indeed, a number of directions outlined in the report of the Program Policy Review Committee (MCU, September 1989) are consistent with the proposals in this report. For example, we share the view of the Committee that MCU should continue to be responsible for program approval and that the approval process should be streamlined. Furthermore, we concur with the Committee's suggestion that designated system-wide programs should not require separate Ministry approval for each college. We suggest that the Ministry seek the advice of CSAC in determining which programs might be so designated.

Concluding notes: We do not underestimate the complexity of developing system-wide program standards and a comprehensive review process. We also realize that some new costs will be involved. But, as we have noted, the credibility of the college system is at stake, and the effort and resources must be forthcoming.

The commitment to enhancing the quality of college programs should find concrete expression as soon as possible. As one of its first initiatives, CSAC should establish two program councils to guide pilot projects over a period of not more than three years. Such projects will provide a clearer picture of how to implement the new system and the costs associated with it. These pilots should be in areas where the interest and co-operation of both internal and external stakeholders have already been demonstrated, as in technology, or where the community of interest is clear and identifiable, as in early childhood education.

In recommending the formation of CSAC, we have concluded that the key areas of program standards and review must be the responsibility of the college community, broadly defined. To suggest otherwise would mean that either such system-wide functions are unnecessary or that a collaborative structure and process are impossible. We believe our recommendations are both sensible and practical. The broad range of stakeholders with whom Vision 2000 has consulted would not endorse the system-wide initiatives recommended here in the absence of the participatory structure for attempting such a significant undertaking.

5

Serving Communities:
A Diversity of Needs

▌5.1 Preamble

Broadly speaking, this chapter is about expanding opportunities. Vision 2000 believes that colleges can — and should — make high-quality, career-oriented education more accessible to a broad range of learners with diverse learning needs. The ultimate aim of improving accessibility is not just to recruit more students; it is to help expand people's educational and employment opportunities, and in so doing, to raise the overall educational and skill level of Ontario's workforce.

The way we foresee the colleges improving accessibility also makes an important statement about the kind of institutions the colleges should be. Access must be equitable: that is, there must be equal opportunity to enrol and succeed in college programs. There must also be an active effort to "screen in" learners who have different levels of educational achievement, who are from various cultural and linguistic backgrounds, who are from different age groups, and who have had different experiences in the labour force. Equitable access goes beyond providing an open door.

The strategies we recommend include improving student success by providing preparatory programming for students who need it in order to benefit from post-secondary programs. We also propose strategies which go beyond helping students to adapt to the requirements of the institution; there must also be institutional transformations to suit different learning styles and needs, particularly those of the adult, part-time learner.

It is important to note that Vision 2000 had a critical choice to make on the issue of access. In addition to (or instead of) recommending system-wide standards for program outcomes in Chapter 4, we could have proposed limitations on access through new entrance standards which would direct a particular student stream into the colleges, while excluding others. Or we might have decided that preparatory or upgrading courses and basic skills training should be outside the mandate of the college system, so that colleges would cater only to those students who are already qualified for post-secondary studies.

We considered those directions, but did not choose them, primarily because we came to understand, through our consultations with those who depend on the colleges and through our research into the social and economic implications of the alternatives, that the colleges should enhance their broad community focus. One of the fundamental strengths of the system is how the colleges provide leadership and support to the economic and social development of the community. The community, including employers, public agencies and community groups, looks to the colleges to meet a variety of needs. We want to build on this community strength.

Renewing the college system must include a firm commitment to the colleges' role in serving a diversity of needs, through effective partnerships with a full range of community constituencies. To do otherwise is to ignore the best available estimates of Ontario's labour market needs. The pressures of a changing global economy, new techniques of production and a critical series of demographic transitions, all reinforce the centrality of using the colleges to invest in the skills of our workforce.

The rationale for increasing educational opportunities for a broad cross-section of the population has a social as well as an economic context. If, as a society, we choose to concentrate mainly on educating the highly skilled worker, and if we choose to ignore the needs of those who have been traditionally disadvantaged, educationally and economically, we risk widening the gulf between the "haves" and the "have-nots."

We risk creating "an 'hour-glass society,' where some enjoy stimulating, well-paid jobs while a large part of the population is confined to dead-end, low-wage jobs — with frequent spells on the unemployment rolls."[27] That kind of society does not fit with the values of Canadian society that have been built up over generations. Ontario's colleges risk becoming contributors to a more polarized society if they do not make concerted efforts to serve those who need them the most.

Equitable access is a matter of fairness — every student should start with a fair chance to succeed, without being encumbered by factors unrelated to his or her ability to benefit from a college education. It is also a matter of right — the Canadian Charter of Rights and Freedoms enshrines the right of every individual to "have an equal opportunity with other individuals to make for himself or herself the life that he or she is able and wishes to have ... without being hindered in or prevented from doing so by discriminatory practices ..."

5.2 Equitable Access

In the past, providing equitable access was not viewed as an important challenge — partly because systemic discrimination was simply not recognized as such, but also because the population from which the colleges drew their students was relatively homogeneous, and expectations of the system were more limited; that is, the colleges were mainly for young, English-speaking, high school

---

[27] Rianne Mahon, "Toward a Highly Qualified Workforce: Improving the Terms of the Equity-Efficiency Trade-Off," in *Colleges and the Changing Economy. Background Papers* (Toronto: Ontario Council of Regents, 1989), p. 15.

graduates who needed full-time career-oriented programs. Those who did not fit the mould were generally assumed to be of peripheral concern.

Today, the communities of Ontario are increasingly diverse and the expectations of the colleges have expanded enormously. Ontario has become more multicultural, and communities with different linguistic and cultural heritages are looking to the colleges for increased opportunities. Persons with physical disabilities are looking to the colleges to adapt programs and services to meet their needs for education and training beyond high school.

Women's groups are looking to the colleges to encourage more women to enter non-traditional occupations; they are also looking for services such as child care to make education more accessible for single parents and others with family responsibilities. Ontario's Francophones are looking to the college system for greater opportunities for linguistic and cultural affirmation. Ontario's aboriginal communities are looking to the colleges for opportunities to design and direct programs for their own people.

The economically disadvantaged, older workers displaced from their jobs, high school dropouts and a host of other groups are looking to the colleges for educational opportunities.

The mission statements of the colleges express their commitment to being open, accessible and responsive community-based institutions. It is certainly not their intention to set up barriers to equitable access. However, it must be recognized that years of focussing on the needs of the typical post-secondary student have left a legacy of systemic barriers for those who do not fit the mould.

Vision 2000 heard widespread concerns from a variety of stakeholders, both inside and outside the system, that there are significant barriers to equitable access which are affecting the ability of colleges to respond to the needs in their communities and the demands of a changing social and economic environment.

Research was conducted for Vision 2000 into both educational and economic participation by persons with specific disabilities, women, people living in poverty, aboriginal peoples, Francophones, older workers in need of retraining, school dropouts, seniors, and members of diverse racial and cultural groups, particularly first-generation immigrants. The general conclusions are that education, training and jobs are *not* equally accessible to all; that the colleges are well placed to contribute further to expanding opportunities; and that in so doing they will help people to better their own lives and to be more productive members of the workforce.

While some individuals may have experienced overt discrimination in the colleges, by far the greatest problem is systemic. Systemic barriers are those which are built into institutional arrangements and procedures; they are not usually conceived or put in place to keep anyone out, but nonetheless result in some people being treated unfairly. These barriers are often visible only to those who are affected by them, and they usually have at least as much to do with what is not in place, as with what is. Systemic barriers also tend to change with changing social and economic conditions. Ironically, the more effective the barriers are, the less likely it is that those who create and maintain them will ever hear about them from those who are affected.

Research conducted for Vision 2000 attempted to identify the major barriers hindering more effective service for underserved groups and individuals. These can be organized under five broad headings: attitudes/policies; physical facilities; support services; organization and structure of programs; and structure and allocation of the system's resource base.

Some of these systemic barriers may affect one particular "special" community or group, while others are more general. For example, physical facilities tend to be a problem for persons with physical disabilities, while inadequate support services and inflexible program structures may affect a wide range of would-be learners, from a parent who cannot afford child care services to a shiftworker who cannot find a skills upgrading course to fit his/her schedule.

Barriers to equitable access may be reflected in under-representation in the college student body. For instance, the proportion of status Indian students in post-secondary education is small relative to participation rates of the rest of the population. Numbers, however, are not the only yardstick.

Women, for example, make up over half the total college student population. Colleges have an important role to play in assisting women to move beyond the historical pattern of labour market segregation. Women earn two-thirds of the average income of men; they are over-represented in occupations such as clerical work, which are traditionally low-paying and vulnerable to the impact of new technologies; and under-represented in management, administration and technical occupations.

There are also certain segments of the female population, such as sole-support mothers living below the poverty line, who may require support services to enable them to go to college. Low income tends to be a common factor among many of those who are underserved. Poverty limits opportunities in all sorts of areas, one of which is education. Many of those who are employment disadvantaged, such as a school dropout who is limited, by lack of skills, to low-level dead-end jobs, have been underserved — and have educational needs that colleges can help address.

Affordability of a college education is a major accessibility issue for students, particularly those from low-income families. College tuition fees are discussed in the context of quality, access and funding trade-offs in Chapter 7.

Perspectives on diverse needs

> What is clear is that those with education and training will have more choices to make. Under current conditions, those with the fewest choices will be women, the disabled, older workers, the poor, visible minorities, Native Peoples, and recent immigrants. Especially with new technologies, the benefits of greater investment in education and training are not restricted to the individuals involved. By expanding educational opportunities, Ontario will have more choices as a province to make.[28]

---

[28] Pat Armstrong and Hugh Armstrong, "Choosing Equity and Prosperity: Access to College and the Ontario Economy," in *Colleges and the Changing Economy. Background Papers* (Toronto: Ontario Council of Regents, 1989), p. 18.

Vision 2000 consulted with a number of "special" communities to hear their concerns about accessibility and equity in the colleges. The following is an overview of the diversity of needs expressed by these constituencies.

Diverse racial and cultural groups: There is increasing evidence to suggest that people from diverse racial and cultural backgrounds (whether they are recent immigrants or have lived in this country all their lives) do not have the same opportunities as others in the job market, and that many of their talents are underused or underdeveloped. Many members of these groups find it difficult to get into educational programs at the college level and have little information on the availability of training opportunities.[29]

A significant proportion of recent immigrants have technical, professional or trade skills or business expertise, but experience difficulty having their credentials recognized here. (See Chapter 6 for a further discussion.) An increasing proportion of recent immigrants do not have English or French literacy skills, and many have little formal education.

All colleges provide English as a Second Language (ESL) courses. Many offer other programs for recent immigrants and are making concerted efforts to reach diverse racial and cultural communities. However, groups consulted by Vision 2000 indicated the need for more language programs and more attention to cultural sensitivities and race relations.

People with disabilities: The Office for Disabled Persons estimates there are 937,000 adults with special needs in Ontario, or almost 13 per cent of the province's adult population. About 18 per cent of the population of people with special needs have some post-secondary education, compared with 33 per cent of the rest of the adult population. Among the youth population, there are growing numbers of students identified as having learning disabilities.

System-wide special needs funding has recently been established for students with physical disabilities, following a task force report to the Council (then Committee) of Presidents. Some colleges provide special services for persons with disabilities such as hearing or visual impairment. Some of these students already attend colleges, but a number of barriers to participation remain.

In general, people with physical and learning disabilities are concerned about the need for more alternative ways of achieving program objectives for diverse learning styles. They believe that there should be system-wide policies to ensure that every college has a basic inventory of technical aids, appropriate supports, outreach activities, services available on evenings and weekends, effective assessment procedures, bridging programs to the workplace, appropriate teacher training, implementation of employment equity, and better funding for special needs.

Vision 2000 agrees that the ultimate aim should be that all colleges accommodate the special needs of students, whatever their specific disability and whatever the program they wish to

---

[29] For more information, see Maureen Hynes, *Access to Potential: A Two-Way Street, and Educational and Training Needs Assessment of Metro Toronto's Diverse Racial and Cultural Communities* (Toronto: George Brown College, 1987).

undertake. However, we must acknowledge that the cost of specialized equipment and services is such that this goal will not be reached in the immediate future. Therefore, we believe the system should explore the sharing of specialized resources for people with disabilities.

The specialization might be by program or by specific disability — one college could specialize in providing business programs for the disabled across a region; or a college might specialize in equipment and services for blind or hearing-impaired students. While we do not see this as the ideal solution, we believe it is a viable option. We discuss other aspects of sharing specialized resources in Chapter 7.

Ontario's Francophones: Francophone participation rates in post-secondary education have historically been about half the rate of the Anglophone population. In 1986, there were 4,463 Francophone students registered in full-time post-secondary programs in the college system. Francophone enrolment represented about 4.6 per cent of total post-secondary enrolment, while Francophones account for about 5.5 per cent of the Ontario population. Fewer than two-thirds of Francophone students were studying in French-language or bilingual programs. There are 63 different programs now provided in the French language across the system (and 300 in English). As noted earlier, the new Francophone college, La Cité collégiale, will open in 1990.

As noted in Chapter 1 of this report, Vision 2000 heard the views of Ontario's Francophones through the Sixth Table, a special group composed of members from each of the study teams and other key Francophone representatives. The group was established to investigate and draft a special report on the educational needs of the Francophone community in the context of Vision 2000's inquiry into the renewal of the college mandate.[30] The Sixth Table recommended there should be a network of French-language colleges to promote the development of the Francophone community's cultural potential.

The report discussed the economic and community mandate of this network of colleges. It highlighted the crucial role that the colleges must play in preparing Francophone students for the labour market of the future, and in fostering the Francophone community's aspirations on the cultural, social and political levels as well. It said the central mission of the colleges is to make the community aware of educational opportunities and to make these opportunities accessible.

Vision 2000 is supportive of the principle that Francophones should be able to participate fully in college education unencumbered by linguistic differences. However, the Minister of Colleges and Universities has announced the creation of two advisory commissions to examine the question of French-language college services in Northern and Central/Southwestern Ontario. He said that the government is committed to improving and promoting French-language education in Ontario. Vision 2000 applauds and respects this consultative initiative and will therefore refrain from premature comment on the need for additional French-language colleges.

---

[30] For further details see Anne Gilbert, "Franco-Ontarian Vision of the Future of the Colleges," in *Additional Perspectives on the College System. Background Papers* (Toronto: Ontario Council of Regents, 1990).

Aboriginal peoples: The participation rate among aboriginal peoples in post-secondary education in Canada has risen substantially in recent years, but it is still only about half that of the non-aboriginal population. Their participation rates in the labour force and average incomes are also well below that of the non-aboriginal population.

Representatives of aboriginal peoples state that education is an inherent aboriginal right, and that aboriginal peoples should have control over education of their own communities. They emphasize the need for programming that is sensitive to their languages and cultures and supportive of their right to self-determination.

The Ministry of Colleges and Universities (MCU) has appointed an Advisory Committee on Native Post-secondary Education. Since the committee's report had not been released at the time of writing this report, Vision 2000 decided not to comment specifically on issues being studied in detail by the advisory group.

Chart 5.1

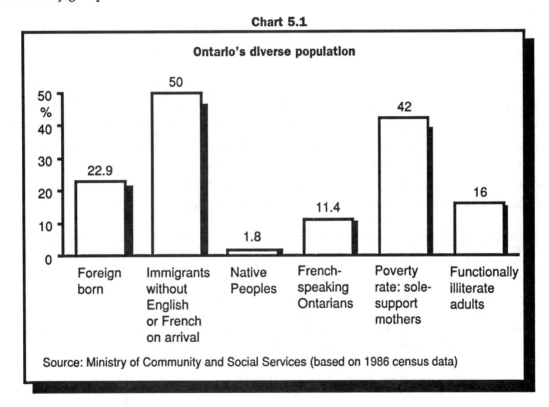

Ontario's diverse population

Source: Ministry of Community and Social Services (based on 1986 census data)

Women: We have already made reference to the inequitable position of women in the workforce. Their average salaries are lower than men's, and they are unevenly distributed across occupational groups; that is, they are clustered in secretarial work, health sciences, community services and social services. Women are also over-represented in the part-time workforce.

Many of the special needs of women are related to issues of poverty. Many low-income women, particularly single parents, cannot afford to work while their children are young because of the cost of child care, and the low wages they would earn in the workforce. Many of these women also have difficulty getting back into the workforce when their children are older because their skills have become obsolete, they have a low level of education or they have no previous employment experience.

Many colleges provide special programs for women in such areas as life skills, employment preparation and entry to non-traditional occupations. Women's groups have identified the need for targeted training and supports, particularly child care and specialized counselling, and bridging and outreach programs to help overcome the barriers facing women.

Implementing educational equity

Providing equitable access for diverse communities means reinforcing the colleges' commitment to equity, strengthening their community development focus and identifying ways to increase participation of a wide range of students, both adults and youth, by being as flexible, innovative and open to change as possible.

Equitable access cannot be a passive principle. It demands active pursuit of measures to remove or counteract the disadvantages faced by potential students.

Much is already happening in the colleges to serve new client groups. But the response of the system as a whole to serving diverse needs has tended to be uneven and sporadic; it has also been too often reactive, rather than proactive. Vision 2000's research and consultation suggests that while many colleges have worked hard to reach out to their communities to meet the growing diversity of needs, much still needs to be done across the system. We believe it is imperative, at this time of renewal, not only for the college system to reaffirm its commitment to equity, but also to have some way whereby those who are underserved may call the system to account.

We have included in our proposed mandate for the Ontario college system a commitment to educational equity, which we have defined as follows:

> Educational equity involves the identification and removal of systemic barriers to educational opportunities that discriminate against women, visible minorities, aboriginal peoples, persons with disabilities, people living in poverty, or members of other groups which have been identified as being underserved with respect to their needs for post-secondary education. Educational equity also involves the implementation of special measures and the application of the concept of reasonable accommodation[31] when these are necessary to achieve and maintain a student group which is representative of the communities served.

While there is a commitment to educational equity in the system's mandate, it is important to make it clear that it is the responsibility of individual colleges to implement policies and monitor progress. In addition, we believe that each college should establish race and ethnic relations policies to promote tolerance and understanding. We also believe that colleges must be committed to

---

[31] The concepts of reasonable accommodation and special measures are described in *Employment and Immigration Canada, Employment Equity: A Guide for Employers* (Minister of Supply and Services Canada, Ottawa, 1987).

employment equity for those groups designated by the Ontario government: persons with disabilities, aboriginal peoples, women, and racial minorities. College staff, boards and committees should reflect the communities of which the colleges are a part.

There is already considerable expertise in the system concerning equity issues. Many colleges have developed their own policies. The groundwork has been laid in identifying barriers to participation by special communities. Specific policies and implementation measures for removing these barriers must be carried out by individual colleges, based on the needs and characteristics of the communities they serve.

Considerable data on students and college personnel will be needed to assist with this process. In Chapter 7 of this report, which deals with strategic planning, we address the issue of systematic data collection and analysis.

Individual colleges must shape their general role to local challenges in order to be relevant to the needs of their communities. Local needs assessment and outreach should involve a range of activities and partnerships with a broad spectrum of local organizations and institutions. Colleges should assess, as part of a regular scanning process, the extent to which their students, employees and programs represent the needs, interests and socio-cultural characteristics of the wider communities in which the colleges are located.

Development and maintenance of partnerships with organizations and institutions from the public, private and non-profit sectors are essential to ensure the colleges are attuned to the needs of their communities. As colleges are seen to be reaching out to diverse communities, the organizations representing different interests and needs will respond.

Colleges are a community resource and as such should contribute to community development. As socially responsible institutions, they should be prepared to play an advocacy role on issues in their communities which affect the potential for educational access, such as policies on child care, literacy, race and ethnic relations and student financial assistance. Many colleges have forged successful partnerships with community groups and have an established community profile on many of these issues.

Since low income tends to be an underlying problem associated with lack of participation in education for many diverse groups, outreach to organizations involved in issues related to poverty should be a priority. While colleges cannot be expected single-handedly to overcome all barriers to education on behalf of low-income people, they should be able to work actively to assist them to deal as effectively as possible with the barriers they face. Colleges should help draw together community groups, trade unions, employers, government agencies and others for a community co-ordinated approach.

The colleges have program advisory committees to help them remain current and relevant to employers' needs. A mechanism is also needed to focus on equity, access and outreach. It could be an advisory committee to the board of governors or a series of committees working with different constituency groups. Whatever methods work for each college, the board should be kept advised on how the college as a whole is responding to the diversity of needs in the local community in terms of equity and access, the development of partnerships with community groups and institutions, the degree of community involvement and participation in college planning, and advocacy activities.

We believe it is important to highlight how colleges are doing things right, and to ensure that the public is made aware of what is happening in the area of equity in the colleges. Thus, each college should be required by MCU to include a specific equity and community outreach section in its annual report to the Minister.

In addition, the Council of Regents (COR) should be charged with the responsibility of producing a report on an annual basis about the system's initiatives to serve diverse communities. This public reporting should serve to reinforce positive activities and call attention to any lack of progress.

COR should also develop guidelines to assist the colleges in developing educational equity policies.

Recommendation 6

Every college should have in place:
- educational equity policies and formally defined measures for implementing and monitoring those policies;
- race and ethnic relations policies to promote tolerance and understanding between peoples of different cultures and races;
- mechanisms to monitor employment equity policies to ensure that college personnel, boards and committees are representative of the diverse communities they serve; and
- mechanisms for building and maintaining effective partnerships with special communities and for advocating on their behalf on issues of educational equity.

Recommendation 7

The Ministry of Colleges and Universities should require every college board of governors to include in the college's annual report to the Minister a specific "Serving Communities" section outlining college activities in the areas of educational equity, race relations, employment equity and community outreach activities.

Recommendation 8

The Council of Regents should develop system-wide guidelines to assist colleges in developing educational equity policies. The Council should also produce and disseminate an annual report on college initiatives in serving communities.

▌5.3 Preparing for Success

Vision 2000 has specifically made access more than an issue of enrolment policy. We have stated in the proposed mandate that students should have the opportunity to succeed, not merely to enrol. What many students need is some preparatory or remedial assistance to allow them to participate successfully in the programs offered at the colleges.

Currently, the colleges serve two categories of underprepared students. One is the adult taking basic skills, literacy, life skills or language training, generally on a short-term basis, in programs usually funded by the federal government (such as the Canada Employment and Immigration Commission), or the provincial government. (The Ministry of Education assumed responsibility for the Ontario Basic Skills programming of the Ministry of Skills Development [MSD] in April 1990.) These students generally do not have an Ontario secondary school graduation diploma; they may be recent immigrants who do not speak English; or, if they do have a diploma, they received it many years ago, and are mature students who are functioning below the Grade 12 level.

The other type of underprepared student is the student just coming out of high school with a secondary school graduation diploma, who is enrolling in a post-secondary vocational program, but who is nevertheless functioning below a Grade 12 level in the basic skills of literacy and numeracy.

The issue has been raised as to whether colleges should be in the business of providing basic skills. It could be argued that students should be sent to the secondary schools or other educational agencies for basic skills upgrading, while the colleges concentrate on post-secondary career-oriented education. However, we believe there are compelling reasons for keeping basic skills/preparatory courses in the colleges for both types of students.

One of the major reasons for having these programs in the colleges is student preference. Many students, recent high school graduates and mature adults alike, may be reluctant to return to high school to do what they would consider to be make-up or catch-up studies, especially if they associate the high school environment with past failure.

For some adult learners, it is a matter of great pride to be "going to college" for a basic skills course. It may also be beneficial for learners to be exposed to the range of other educational opportunities which they could pursue at college after they have completed a basic skills course. In fact, encouraging students to continue learning should be a key outcome of adult basic education.

Another good reason for keeping these programs in the colleges is that many colleges have had great success with adult basic education programs, both as direct providers and as brokers for community groups seeking support for literacy or language training from funders. Some colleges are also engaged in train-the-trainer programs for basic skills education.

In addition, employers will be looking increasingly to the colleges to provide a variety of workplace or work-related training. Part of that demand will be for adult basic education for employees, perhaps combined with some specific skills training.

In the case of post-secondary students, providing preparatory courses at the colleges can be justified on the grounds that it facilitates tailoring the content and scheduling of these courses to the post-secondary programs in which these students are enrolled. This is particularly important because academic underpreparedness has been identified as a major reason why many students drop out of college. One college which followed the outcome of college post-secondary students who were reading below the Grade 10 level determined that about half of them dropped out before graduation; another 11 per cent persisted, but were ineligible for graduation.

Others argue against the inclusion of preparatory courses in the colleges. First, they suggest that offering this type of assistance to high school graduates implies that the secondary schools are inadequate. Second, they argue that offering such access courses undermines the status of a post-secondary institution. Vision 2000 does not concur with either of these last two arguments.

The first viewpoint does not accurately reflect the performance of our secondary school system. Since 1976/77, the enrolment rate of 19-year-olds in Ontario's college and university systems has increased 50 per cent, from a rate of 26 per cent in 1976/77 to 39 per cent in 1988/89. With such a large increase, it would have been very surprising if the issue of underprepared students had not arisen in our colleges and universities. In addition, the changing ethnic composition of Ontario's population has meant that for an increasing number of students, English or French is not their first language.

With respect to the second viewpoint, rather than diminishing the status of college programs, the expansion of preparatory courses would serve to emphasize the high priority colleges give to increasing accessibility, reducing student attrition rates, and enhancing students' abilities to meet high program standards.

The allocation of more resources to the colleges for the training of these underprepared students will provide a valuable social and economic return. This is reinforced by changing demographics. The population and labour force will soon be growing at roughly the same rates, whereas for the last several decades the rate of labour force growth has been much higher than that of the population. As a result, future economic growth will increasingly depend on raising the skill levels of the existing labour force and future labour force entrants, some of whom will go to college. These conditions give added significance to measures which will increase post-secondary enrolment and completion rates.

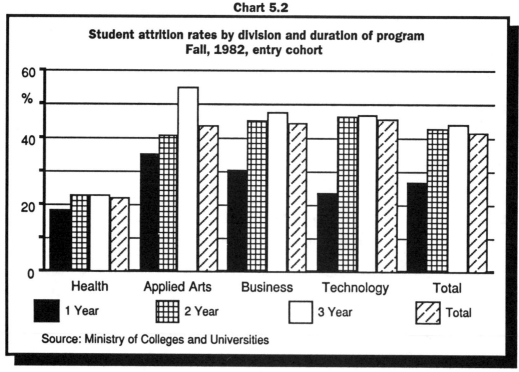

Chart 5.2

Note: Attrition rates (drop out rates) for those entering the college system from 1976 to 1984 were examined. The attrition rates of the 1982 college entry cohort are typical of the rates throughout this period.

Chapter 5 Serving Communities: A Diversity of Needs

If colleges are to live up to their goal of serving communities, providing basic skill and preparatory courses should be part of what they do. If colleges are to be learner-driven institutions which support lifelong learning, they should be open to all learners at all levels of educational achievement. The adult student taking basic skills training may eventually enrol in a post-secondary program. And if colleges are genuinely committed to access with success, preparatory assistance to high school graduates enrolled in post-secondary programs is a necessity.

The high school graduate

Currently, the college system does not systematically collect and analyze data on the literacy and numeracy levels of the students entering post-secondary programs. Some colleges require students to take reading and mathematics achievement tests or provide writing samples; others do not.

It is essential for colleges to know at what level students are reading and at what level their math skills are. Otherwise, many students are left on their own to flounder in college programs for which they are inadequately prepared. That is unfair to students, many of whom become discouraged and drop out, and to faculty, who must cope with classes in which there is substantial variation in literacy and numeracy skills.

We recognize that assessing every student on entry to college may mean testing thousands of students at every college every year. However, some colleges are already doing considerable testing. And it may be that not every applicant with a high school diploma needs to take a test or do a writing sample. If there are co-operative links between a college and a particular high school or group of schools, the college may not feel it is necessary to test graduates of those schools because the outcome standards of the schools are known to the college. The need for assessment of an individual student should be at the discretion of the college. However, we believe every college should have the required assessment services in place.

We see assessment services as valuable contact points between the students and the college at the time of admission. It may lead some students who are unsure about their program choice to placement counselling. It may lead others into preparatory courses. The process should be a matter of "screening in" not "screening out," and it should have a significant impact on student success rates.[32]

Vision 2000 obtained data from three colleges on the reading levels of students during the 1981-86 period. The results from these colleges indicated that between between 17 and 36 per cent of incoming first-year students were reading below the Grade 10 level. A 1989 survey by the Ontario College Heads of Language provides some corroboration, indicating that almost 40 per cent of incoming students with a Grade 12 diploma are reading at the Grade 10 level or below.

---

[32] In the next chapter, we discuss a mechanism for providing evaluation and credit for prior learning and experience for those who do not come to college directly from high school. If they choose, this could be another avenue for prospective students to be assessed before enrolling in college.

There are varying opinions as to what level of literacy is required in order to be successful in college programs. Many in the colleges believe that Grade 10 is the minimum level necessary if students are to avoid having serious problems in comprehending text material in their courses.

A recent national literacy study lends support to the notion that a sizeable percentage of secondary school graduates may be experiencing real difficulty in post-secondary studies as a result of deficiencies in basic skills. The Southam News study, *Literacy in Canada* (1987), found that 17 per cent of Canadian high school graduates are functional illiterates — "those whose reading and writing and number skills are not sufficient to get by in everyday life."

The college community is certainly aware that a significant number of entrants have less than adequate literacy skills. However, there is no explicit government policy on how colleges should meet these students' needs, nor is funding provided explicitly for the upgrading of basic skills.

If a college chooses to provide preparatory/remedial courses, the funds usually have to come from general operating revenues, thus diverting funds from regular programs and services. Some colleges provide clinics for students reading below a Grade 10 level; at least one college makes the course mandatory, based on testing of first-year entrants. Other colleges provide tutorial assistance for mathematics, language and study skills, either in learning centres or in a specific course.

Some colleges use "back-door" means to obtain some funding for remedial courses for post-secondary students. For example, some colleges have assigned two functions to their General Arts and Science (GAS) post-secondary programs, which are funded by MCU. The first function is career exploration and general education, the original (and approved) purpose of most GAS programs. The second function is remedial and preparatory work, for which colleges have not obtained explicit approval from MCU.

Colleges may also enrol these students in adult basic upgrading courses funded by Canada Employment and Immigration Commission (CEIC). But space limitations, as well as some reluctance on the part of secondary school graduates to enrol in these courses, limit their participation.

We estimate that the cost of upgrading the literacy level by one grade for one quarter of the first-year, post-secondary students in the system would be in excess of $8 million per year in faculty time, or approximately $650 per student per grade level.[33] To the extent that underprepared secondary school graduates require an improvement of more than one grade level, the costs would be correspondingly higher. The cost of upgrading the numeracy levels of incoming post-secondary students has not been estimated, as we have not been able to examine data relevant to this issue.

We do not have aggregate data on current college expenditures on literacy and numeracy upgrading. However, it is clear that there is no consistency in the availability of these programs across the system. It is also apparent that there is a pressing need for preparatory and remedial

---

[33] This cost estimate is based on student-teacher ratios of 15:1 and 100 hours of instruction per student. Some suggest that more efficient learning can take place in individualized programs which might allow for higher ratios. Others, however, suggest that lower ratios will be necessary to assist learners at this level.

courses for a significant number of students, and that this need is unlikely to disappear in the near future. In fact, future needs could increase considerably if post-secondary enrolment rates rise.

We have concentrated on literacy because of its crucial impact on students' abilities to comprehend study material, but it should also be noted that some students also lack specific prerequisites (e.g. chemistry or senior level high school mathematics) for the program they wish to undertake, and they look to the college to help them meet these requirements. Since prerequisites vary from college to college, even in programs with the same title, it is difficult for students to ensure they will have the right secondary school courses unless they choose their college and program early in their high school career. In the next chapter of this report, we suggest improvements in links between the secondary school and college systems which may alleviate this problem. We also suggest how a system for assessing prior learning will help adults receive credit for experiential learning.

We have concluded, based on our own research and on consultations with the college community, that there are two major gaps: the college system does not have the necessary assessment services in place, and it is not providing remedial and preparatory courses to the extent required by underprepared students. The lack of explicit government policy and funding for underprepared, post-secondary students has contributed to these conditions. However, it is encouraging that MCU recently announced some experimental funding in this area.

Recommendation 9

> Every college should, where necessary, conduct assessments of the literacy and numeracy levels of applicants to college credential programs for the purpose of appropriate placement. The need for assessment of an individual student should be at the discretion of the college.

Recommendation 10

> Ontario's colleges should provide preparatory courses designed to meet the needs of those with a secondary school diploma or equivalent seeking admission to college credential programs. These courses may be offered in conjunction with local school boards.

Recommendation 11

> The Ministry of Colleges and Universities should provide explicit funding to the colleges for preparatory courses in a manner consistent with the funding of college post-secondary programs.

Adult basic education

It is estimated that one in every six working Canadians is functionally illiterate. Illiteracy is eroding the economic security of workers and adding cost burdens to employers. It can also have a devastating effect on the development of the individual, since not being able to read or write often isolates people from their communities.

It is estimated that almost all jobs require some reading, and two hours of reading per day at a Grade 10 level is common. A 1985 survey of managers in the automotive parts industry revealed that 29 per cent found their current workers' literacy skills inadequate, and 36 per cent said their workers' mathematical skills were insufficient.[34] The Canadian Business Task Force on Literacy has estimated direct costs of illiteracy to be $4 billion annually.

The Economic Council of Canada has noted that the hazard of unemployment associated with low levels of educational attainment increased considerably from 1975 to 1988.[35] The Economic Council and the Premier's Council, among others, are warning that in the future even higher levels of skills in the labour force will be required to meet global competition and adapt to technological change.

There have been a variety of basic education programs for adults. They include those programs designated as literacy or basic skills, including Ontario Basic Skills (OBS), Adult Basic Education (ABE), English as a Second Language (ESL), English for Special Purposes (ESP), Basic Training for Skills Development (BTSD) and a variety of programs targeted at, for example, high school dropouts.

The federal and provincial governments are involved in funding, as are local school boards, employers, labour and some community agencies. Significant sums have been provided directly to the colleges by the federal government through CEIC for ESL and literacy upgrading activities under the BTSD program. The Ontario MSD has provided funding through OBS for college-based, workplace and community-based literacy activities. Basic education is usually a significant component of MSD's targeted programs such as Futures, adjustment programs for older workers and those returning to the labour force (e.g. Basic Job Readiness Training), and programs for women, aboriginal people and other targeted groups.

In addition, several other Ontario ministries provide funding, including Education, Community and Social Services, Citizenship, and Correctional Services. Local school boards fund, from local tax levies, programs in their schools and in other community facilities. Both labour and employers are making direct contributions to basic education activities through workplace programs; in some cases, they are providing the training directly, as in the Metro Toronto Labour Council programs. A number of not-for-profit agencies and some private suppliers have received funding for basic education programs (e.g. Frontier College, John Howard Society).

Given the diversity of potential learners and circumstances and the extent of demand, we believe that maintaining a variety of suppliers of adult basic education is the most effective approach. There are benefits to having different locations and modes of instruction to reach different learners.

The scope and seriousness of the illiteracy problem is such that colleges could not possibly meet all the demand for adult basic skills upgrading. The need for an expanded effort to address this social and economic problem is urgent. We believe colleges should remain one of the prime suppliers of adult basic education, but they should not be made responsible for solving the illiteracy challenge facing society in general. That is the responsibility of governments, not the colleges.

---

[34] Ministry of Skills Development, *Literacy — The Basics of Growth* (Toronto: Queen's Printer, 1988).

[35] Economic Council of Canada, *Good Jobs, Bad Jobs. Employment in the Service Economy. A statement by the Economic Council of Canada* (Ottawa: Ministry of Supply and Services, 1990).

Vision 2000 believes that meeting our literacy goals will require improvement in co-ordination of services and funding by government. Multiple funders and multiple service providers are not a problem; it is the fragmentation of effort which is hurting the effectiveness of service. Providers complain they are spending increasing amounts of time and energy trying to access funding through a variety of structures — time and energy that would be better spent on their clients.

One encouraging aspect of the work in this field is the growing number of partnerships, which indicate the kind of co-operation that is possible.[36] To increase the number and effectiveness of such activities, Vision 2000 believes it is necessary to co-ordinate policy and planning and to provide increased funding, on a stable footing. We also want to see an effective mechanism for local initiatives. While many providers strive to accommodate more of those in need, the scope of basic education problems requires that targets be set and providers be evaluated as to how effectively and efficiently communities are meeting their goals.

Given its primary constitutional responsibilities in the area of education, we believe it is the provincial government that should take responsibility for providing a focus for accountability of funding and better co-ordination of supply. It should be emphasized, however, that we are not recommending that the province take on responsibility for providing all the funding or all the service. However, the province should see that this urgent issue is addressed in a coherent way.

One possible approach that should be examined is the creation or designation of a provincial agency or department with responsibility for the ongoing co-ordination of policy, planning and funding of adult basic education programs. This provincial agency could establish local adult basic education committees, with representation from providers and funders, to determine the nature of local needs and the ability of various providers, individually and in partnerships, to address those needs; it could also recommend appropriate funding levels. To introduce more stability and predictability into funding, the provincial body could allocate funds to the local committees on a three-year cycle to address agreed-upon needs.

Recommendation 12

> The college system should continue to be a major provider of adult basic education.

Recommendation 13

> The provincial government should accept responsibility for the co-ordination of policy, planning and increased funding of adult basic education programs in Ontario.

---

[36] Five examples are described in the report by the Association of Canadian Community Colleges, *Literacy in the Colleges and Institutes* (1989).

5.4 Colleges and Fee-for-Service Activity

In this section, we focus on issues related to those fee-for-service activities that provide training beyond the level of adult basic education. Much of this activity is non-post-secondary training in narrowly defined job-specific skills; it is usually of short duration (i.e., one year or less) and involves a variety of purchasers, including both the provincial and federal governments, employers and international agencies. Colleges' fee-for-service activities account for approximately 20 per cent of total college revenues, with significant variation among the colleges. The largest proportion of these revenues comes from the federal government through the Canadian Jobs Strategy (CJS) program and from the provincial government through MSD. Direct employer-sponsored training is estimated to account for only three per cent of total college revenues, with far greater potential than has been tapped to date.

In this section, we discuss fee-for-service in the context of responding to the needs of employers and their workers. We also discuss issues relating to fee-for-service training purchased with public dollars by the federal and provincial government.

Responding to the needs of workers and employers

One of the main pressures affecting colleges in the future will be the increasing demand to upgrade and update the skills of those already in the labour force. In addition to our own consultations, we note that the Premier's Council has focussed considerable attention on the need to develop more extensive training opportunities in order to increase the productive capacities of our workforce. There is great scope for the colleges to serve increasing numbers and types of employers seeking to meet their employees' skill development needs. But this expanded role will occur only if the colleges can make the necessary adjustments to enable them to respond effectively.

Consultations by Vision 2000 with a broad range of sectoral groups, including manufacturing, information, social services, finance, hospitality and resources, confirm that most expect demands on the colleges to increase from their sector. "Upgrading and retraining are key, and the needs are not being met very well. College and industry can easily cooperate to improve in this area."[37] We anticipate that recommendations forthcoming from the Premier's Council will increase the level of investment in labour force education. We feel strongly that the colleges must be directly involved in the planning and implementation of these initiatives. Vision 2000's experience reflects an impressive degree of willingness, on the part of employers, labour and educators, to work co-operatively.

---

[37] Audrey Gill, "Role of the Colleges in the Changing Economy: Report on Consultations," *Colleges and the Changing Economy. Background Papers* (Toronto: Ontario Council of Regents, 1989), p. 32.

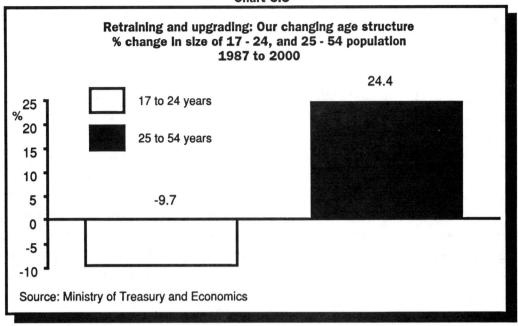

Chart 5.3

Retraining and upgrading: Our changing age structure
% change in size of 17 - 24, and 25 - 54 population
1987 to 2000

24.4

%
- 25
- 20
- 15
- 10
- 5
- 0
- -5
- -10

17 to 24 years

25 to 54 years

-9.7

Source: Ministry of Treasury and Economics

Sharing the investment while resisting inappropriate public subsidies: The fee-for-service area is one which Vision 2000 believes will, and should, become a more important function of the colleges. To ensure that that the public interest is well served, as well as the interests of employers and workers, there should be carefully developed guidelines governing the colleges' fee-for-service activities. Currently, there are some concerns and confusion about the existing ground rules; in addition, changing circumstances may require further development of fee-for-service guidelines.

Future guidelines need to reflect the new partnerships which will be required to meet emerging needs. Broadly speaking, a distinction must be drawn between training provided at the colleges which serves the the broader public interest and that which serves only narrow private interests.

Guidelines might distinguish between two types of activities: those courses which are counted as a credit in a credential program and those which are not. The former would be funded by MCU through the formula allocation for credential programs, with the purchaser paying only the standard tuition fees which currently represent 12 to 25 per cent of the costs. In order to receive formula funding, those enrolled as trainees (be they government or employer-sponsored students) would need to meet the normal course entry requirements, and the course would need to be available to the general public. Those courses which do not provide a credit toward a credential program would be purchased from the college at full cost by the client.

Strict application of the credit/non-credit distinction would allow the MCU operating grant to be dedicated to supporting activities leading to a college credential, including preparatory and remedial courses. We expect that the demands from employers for greater emphasis on generic skills, coupled with our recommendation in Chapter 4 for more emphasis on generic skills in courses which count as a credit toward a college credential, will result in an increasing number of credit courses being of interest to employers and their workers. Given that these courses would assist individuals in becoming more employable by providing portable skills, it appears to be in the public interest to fund these offerings directly, whether the client enrols as an individual or is sponsored by an employer, union or other community group. Thus, to the extent that sponsors seek such courses, there would exist a *de facto* sharing of costs between the public, as represented by MCU, and the sponsor.

Basing MCU funding support solely on whether a course is credit or non-credit does, however, raise several issues. For example, what are termed "part-time, vocational, non-credit" courses are now funded through the MCU operating grant, with participants paying a standard fee which represents approximately 25 per cent of the costs. If the distinction between credit and non-credit courses were applied literally, these courses would no longer receive support from the MCU operating grant. However, enrolment in non-credit vocational courses currently represents an important area of college activity, with about eight percent of the MCU operating grant being used to support these courses. Such courses, while not necessarily focussing to any great extent on portable or developmental skills, meet the needs or desires of many workers, employers and interested citizens. The issue of whether non-credit, vocational courses should be funded through the operating grant requires careful study.

Another area which requires examination is the public's role in supporting courses provided by the colleges which have been customized to meet specific, narrowly defined needs of employers and unions. Under current guidelines, such courses are not eligible for funding support from from MCU; nor would they be eligible if funding support were restricted to credit courses. In general, we believe there should be more generic skills content in non-credit courses, including those which are customized to meet specific needs of employers and unions. If the offerings included a greater emphasis on generic skills, it might be in the public interest for the government to provide some public subsidy — not necessarily as large as that which would be provided to credit courses — to encourage greater participation in such training opportunities.

There is also the question of whether funding should be provided when, for example, enrolment in a class of a credit course is limited to employees of a particular firm, with the class perhaps being offered at the firm's location of business. Under current guidelines, if the section is identical in content to other sections of the same course which are available to the public, it is somewhat unclear as to whether the employer-sponsored class is eligible for MCU funding.

It may be desirable to develop guidelines which explicitly allow for MCU funding of a section of a post-secondary credit course which is entirely composed of trainees designated by an employer. In some instances the unit costs of the employer's class may exceed the unit costs of those sections provided to the general public; some faculty time may be taken up travelling to the employer's location or the class size of the employer's section may be smaller than that of other sections. Funding support could be limited to that provided on average to other sections of the same course which are available to the public.

From the foregoing discussion it is clear that there are several complex but important issues related to public subsidies and fee-for-service training. It will be important to clarify the rules and reinforce the distinction between those activities which are appropriately eligible for public funding and those which are not. In addition, where public dollars are spent, there should also be accountability procedures and the guidelines governing fee-for-service training should be widely distributed and understood. The aim of developing new guidelines is not to discourage fee-for-service activity by the colleges; on the contrary, it is to ensure that there are guidelines which allow the colleges to meet future demand and to increase the public benefit.

Recommendation 14

An ad hoc task force on fee-for-service training by colleges should be established by the Council of Regents to advise the Minister on policy guidelines which would foster the colleges' role in meeting the training needs of the existing workforce in a manner consistent with public policy goals.

Increasing colleges' flexibility: Another concern is the need for greater flexibility in the scheduling and location of training. In order to be viable suppliers of fee-for-service training, colleges will need to focus on both quality and flexibility.

It will be necessary for colleges to schedule more weekend and summer courses and to find ways of integrating sponsored students into the regular daytime courses of the colleges. More intensive training courses must be developed — ones which last two or three weeks but which address the same objectives as regular college courses. Colleges must increase the amount of training they provide off-campus, for example, in the workplace. And colleges must provide this increased flexibility in a cost-efficient and quality-effective manner.

Achieving these changes will require a commitment on the part of college administrators, faculty and support staff. According to some of those consulted by Vision 2000, the current collective agreement's provisions governing workload of college faculty are perceived to constrain the ability of colleges to supply fee-for-service activity. The provisions concerning faculty workload should be examined with a view to providing greater flexibility in deploying staff without increasing the overall workload of faculty. Vision 2000 respects and supports the collective bargaining process and encourages the parties to the collective agreement to explore creative means to enhance the effectiveness of college fee-for-service activity.

Recommendation 15

Beginning from the current collective agreement, the parties should seek ways to facilitate the colleges' ability to provide fee-for-service activities.

We believe that the fee-for-service educational activities offered by colleges can meet the increasing needs of a variety of clients, by providing high quality training in a timely and flexible manner. However, if colleges are to provide more fee-for-service courses to employers, they must let the private sector know what they have to offer. The colleges should market their abilities to provide generic and job-specific skills training. This is important from at least two perspectives.

First, it is essential for the overall well-being of Ontario's labour force that more workers receive additional training. Many employers and employees will seek training on their own initiative, but we expect there will remain significant numbers who are not committed to investing in training. These people may need to be convinced to undertake the necessary investments. Marketing the successes and benefits of training courses is one means by which increasing numbers of employers can become aware of the crucial role training can play in the economic viability of their firms.

Second, if highly qualified college faculty are to commit themselves to the development and delivery of this training, they will require some assurance that there will be reasonably stable employment; that is, they will require that their college make a consistent and sustained effort to attract clients who sponsor fee-for-service activity.

 Recommendation 16

> **Each college, in conjunction with faculty and staff, should develop strategies for establishing long-term relationships with local fee-for-service clients such as employers and labour organizations.**

One effective strategy may be to develop exchanges between colleges and local employers, whereby faculty undertake work placements in local business and industry, and employees of these firms provide some instruction at the college. This would assist faculty in keeping current and provide individuals in business and industry with an opportunity to experience first-hand the wide range of training opportunities available at a college.

Another strategy may be to develop more co-operative programs for full-time post-secondary students. Not only will the students benefit, but employers and employees will develop a greater awareness of the training provided by colleges through their contacts with these students. These co-operative activities should serve to develop greater interest in college courses and programs.

A more direct strategy would involve colleges developing co-sponsorship arrangements with local associations, employers and unions. Such arrangements would involve the sharing of costs and expertise in delivery of training to workers. As with the entrepreneurship centres which have been established at selected colleges and universities, co-sponsorships would require government funding support to enable colleges to enter into these arrangements.

Public spending on training

Public expenditures and public institutions: An important factor in the current skills training environment is that fee-for-service expenditures by governments have been increasingly directed toward private suppliers of training, including both not-for-profit and profit-oriented organizations.[38] This trend represents, in part, recent changes in the philosophy of government and, to a certain extent, general concerns about the effectiveness of public institutions. Regardless of the motivation, this trend has had important practical effects on the colleges.

The shift in funding allocation has occurred principally through the federal government's use of intermediary bodies such as the Local Advisory Committees (LACs) or the provincially-established

---

[38] We are not referring to training which public employers purchase for their employees.

Community Industrial Training Committees (CITCs) and direct funding of private suppliers of training. Where funds are dispensed through intermediary bodies such as LACs or CITCs rather than directly from the federal government, colleges compete with other suppliers of training for these funds.

Since the introduction of the CJS in 1985/86, an increasing proportion of the training dollars allocated by the federal government has gone to other suppliers of training. By 1988/89, almost 10 per cent of federal training dollars were being allocated to non-college suppliers of training. In addition, since the introduction of CJS, there has been a 14 per cent decline in total federal training expenditures in Ontario. This decline, coupled with the increased emphasis on private trainers, resulted in a 20 per cent decline (in constant dollars) in federal revenues — direct and indirect — flowing to the colleges between 1985/86 and 1988/89.

The negative impact of these policy and funding changes on the colleges would have been considerably more severe if private suppliers of educational services had been in a position to meet the demand. Nevertheless, we believe that policy-makers have not adequately considered the extent to which the CJS approach undermines our public training infrastructure. It is particularly important to assess the implications of redirecting funds away from the colleges at a time when the conflict between limited budgets and growing socio-economic demands are already straining their viability.

Vision 2000 is aware of the widespread concern that public dollars be spent wisely, with the aim of getting the highest-quality services at the lowest possible cost. We share this concern and believe that the pursuit of "good value" for public investment must take into account both the nature of public educational goals and the impact of funding changes on the ability of public institutions to meet these goals.

Our perspective on this issue has been influenced by three factors.

First, it is important to distinguish between the expectations of public and private purchasers of educational services. The perceptions and attitudes of the key constituencies consulted by Vision 2000, such as business, labour and the college community, indicate a clear recognition that private spending on education will be allocated in keeping with private needs and objectives. Equivalent support is offered for the proposition that public funds be devoted to sustaining the public institutions charged with instilling the broad-based knowledge needed to be a good citizen and a capable worker. Respect for these different roles is accompanied by a clear recognition that funding levels must be adequate to assure the integrity of public institutions. There is a similar consensus on the need for a greater amount of privately funded, employer-sponsored training.

A second factor to be considered is the inherent difficulty and expense of realizing the goals of public educational institutions. Providing knowledge which is portable from job to job in today's complex economy and which serves to improve the contributions people can make to society requires significant and sustained investment in teachers, infrastructure and students. Canadians have traditionally believed that it is the role of public institutions to provide this type of public good and have therefore been willing to provide the funding needed to reach these social goals.

Finally, a third factor that must be taken into account is the ability of public institutions to sustain a focus on social goals when funding decisions are being made on the basis of short-run lowest-cost criteria. In some circumstances, it is best to select the lowest-cost, quick-return investments. However, to use such criteria in the realm of public education is to subject past investments in public institutions to excessive rates of depreciation and to risk undermining Ontario's future by failing to provide the kind of education its citizens need.

Given these factors, Vision 2000 supports the general principle that public funds for educational purposes should be used to support public institutions. In applying this principle, it is important to recognize that there are a wide variety of circumstances in which partnerships between public and private suppliers of training will serve the public interest. At present, some good examples involve joint initiatives in the area of adult basic education — the Metro Toronto Labour Education and Skills Training Centre works in conjunction with George Brown College on curriculum development and program evaluation, and a number of successful community literacy projects receive funding through local boards of education.

Colleges should be encouraged to form partnerships with other trainers when special community needs indicate that such a solution is necessary. If public institutions are not able to meet the needs of the community, then public funds ought to be provided to the appropriate educational supplier and attempts should be made to form, wherever and whenever possible, working relationships with public institutions.

 Recommendation 17

> **The Ontario government should adopt the principle that public funds, aimed at covering the costs associated with skills training, should be used primarily to support programs provided by or in conjunction with public institutions, including colleges.**

Ensuring public accountability: One of the challenges for government in attempting to increase private-sector investment in training is to ensure that publicly funded institutions are not arbitrarily excluded and that public policy objectives are not compromised. Our concern is to ensure effective means for realizing public policy goals and maintaining accountability for public funds.

The movement toward involving more private-sector trainers and employers has, in certain instances, led to circuitous and possibly inappropriate funding arrangements. For example, one college's private foundation received federal funding that was earmarked for private trainers. This college's foundation, in order to provide the training, "subcontracted" with the college for the teaching. In this example, both the college and the agency working on behalf of the federal government found it necessary to resort to this kind of indirect contract in order to offer the program. Although the federal government may, as a matter of principle, want to privatize training, this and other examples suggest that the private sector suppliers of training may be unable or unwilling to provide appropriate courses. In such cases, it does not make sense to arbitrarily limit the participation of public institutions.

Similar problems in realizing public policy goals can arise when an employer is given public money to undertake private training. An inappropriate allocation of public funds occurs when a significant portion of the money needed to train a firm's employees is used for equipment (in one reported case, 70 per cent) without any binding commitment to offer training on a continuing basis to these employees or to individuals outside the firm. In such cases, it is unclear how the broader public interest is being served.

From the taxpayers' perspective, two questions must be asked. Is this training valuable enough to the employer to warrant an investment without the public subsidy? And, equally important, is this type of public subsidy — lacking in accountability or commitments on the part of the recipient of public funds to provide ongoing training — an efficient way to use scarce public resources?

We believe that more effective accountability mechanisms should be introduced to ensure that public funds are expended in the public interest when they are supporting employers' training efforts. Vision 2000 strongly supports the efforts of policy-makers, including the Premier's Council, to introduce new institutional mechanisms for co-ordinating the overall resources devoted to training, both public and private. And we share the view that employers should take a more proactive role in ensuring that their employees receive the training or retraining they require. However, we perceive a difficulty in ensuring public accountability in training if programs are conducted without any involvement of public educational institutions.

Training is expected to become more important in the future and may well consume an increasing proportion of public funds. There will be a growing need to provide assurance that the use of public funds is serving public policy objectives. We expect that, as a result of the deliberations of the Premier's Council, the Ontario government will be proposing initiatives aimed at increasing the resources devoted to educating the labour force. Therefore, we direct the following recommendation to the Province.

 Recommendation 18

In order to assure public accountability, any provincial body designated to foster more skills training should include employer and labour representatives and educators, and should produce a public, bi-annual report which:

- describes the training activities receiving public funds;
- shows the distribution of public funds (including federal funds allocated in Ontario) among the providers of training, be they public, private or joint activities;
- evaluates the effectiveness of such training, including an assessment of both quality and cost; and
- identifies training needs which are not being met and which require greater investment.

5.5 The Part-Time Learner

The future that Vision 2000 foresees for the colleges is one in which increasing numbers of adult learners, some of whom have never had any experience with post-secondary education, will be turning to the colleges for educational opportunities. Across the college system, changes are necessary to recognize the importance of the adult learner, who will probably be interested in part-time education or in short episodes of full-time learning.

The estimated 560,000 students taking part-time studies outnumber full-time post-secondary students by almost six to one; yet the colleges are generally perceived to be geared primarily to the needs of the full-time student. The peripheral status of the part-time student body is evidenced in program and service orientation and funding.

Vision 2000 considered the findings of *The Barriers Project* (Confederation College, 1989), in which educators from 31 colleges across Canada identified barriers to part-time learning opportunities in their institutions. The project report, released in 1989, stated that "success with full-time clients has blinded decision-makers from full acceptance of the needs of part-time clients."[39]

All of the colleges in the study shared common concerns about improved conditions for part-time learners. They cited the need to provide alternative times and locations for program delivery, to make part-time learning opportunities a responsibility of the entire college, to market these opportunities effectively, to provide the same services to part-time students that are provided to full-time students, and to develop systems for the assessment of prior learning accomplishments.

Vision 2000 believes that the system must break out of old approaches and formats in order to be more relevant to the needs of people who are not attending school full-time. Courses are now over-whelmingly classroom-based and time-defined. We want to develop a system in which it is commonplace for students to be able to select instructional units from a menu of college courses, accumulate a certain number of units which would add up to what is traditionally considered a course, and earn a college program credential after completing a series of these courses. The units would be based on outcomes, rather than defined by the number of weeks spent in a classroom. And they would not necessarily have to be provided in the traditional institutional setting.

We recognize that introducing greater flexibility across the system will require extensive work on curriculum development, human resource development and alternative delivery forms. We address these issues in Chapter 8 of this report. It is the view of Vision 2000 that this is the direction in which the college system should be heading, and that it is time to make the investment.

---

39 Confederation College, *The Barriers Project* (Thunder Bay, Ontario: Confederation College of Applied Arts and Technology, 1989), p. 1.

More flexible program choices will improve opportunities for all learners, but they will be particularly beneficial for part-time adult learners, most of whom must fit their educational pursuits into their work and family responsibilities. However, further measures are needed to assist and encourage the part-time learner. Many college services, such as career counselling and child care, are available only during the day. Course availability and selection are more limited for part-time students.

To focus attention on the needs of the part-time learner, we propose that every college appoint an advisory committee on part-time learning. This committee would have college-wide responsibilities; it would not be limited to any particular program; and it would provide advice to the college on adapting programs and services to the needs of part-time learners. There are a number of initiatives which colleges could take in the short term to improve opportunities. For example, early childhood education programs which include demonstration/instructional child care centres could be organized to provide evening services for part-time students. Other departments which provide student-operated college services under faculty supervision could be similarly structured to provide evening services.

However, in order to ensure better programming and services for part-time learners, funding should be adjusted. Vision 2000 heard a number of concerns about how funding is tied to an outdated vision of what the colleges should be doing.

Part-time students taking courses during the daytime generate approximately 25 per cent less grant funding per instructional hour than do full-time students in the same classroom. Only part of this difference is offset by the part-time fee, which in relative terms is higher than the full-time fee. The differential in grant funding is largely due to part-time students generating funding as if they are taught by part-time teachers, who receive less per teaching hour than full-time teachers. This funding differential puts part-time students at a disadvantage in seeking admission to day courses.

It must be recognized that a full-time student, purchasing several courses at once, provides certain economies of scale in terms of administration and scheduling, for example. Therefore, to ensure equal treatment of part-time and full-time day students, it may be necessary to adjust funding so that the part-time student generates, on a pro-rated basis, more revenue than a full-time student.

It is also a concern that some colleges may be emphasizing revenue generation in their evening part-time classes, and not reinvesting the profits in the part-time operation, but rather using them to subsidize their full-time programs. As a result, colleges implicitly place restrictions on the range of services provided to part-time students. These restrictions may apply to support services; they may also affect the flexibility of scheduling, location and size of part-time classes.

If the colleges are to become more responsive to part-time learners, then there must be changes in provincial funding policies as well as the manner in which colleges internally allocate funds in order to facilitate and encourage this reshaping of priorities.

Other issues related to the part-time learner are addressed in other chapters of this report. Chapter 6 discusses fair assessment for prior learning, including credit for life experiences and procedures for acceptance of foreign credentials; and Chapter 8 provides recommendations on human resource development which will provide opportunities for college faculty and staff to develop strategies for teaching the adult learner.

 Recommendation 19

To better support the needs of part-time learners:

- **every college should provide a variety of flexible learning opportunities, through varying educational methods, greater use of customized instructional methods, off-campus teaching locations, variable course entrance and completion dates, and other innovative approaches to delivery of relevant and adult-based programming for part-time learners;**
- **each college should have an advisory committee on part-time learning; and**
- **provincial funding and the internal allocation of college revenues should explicitly recognize the nature and importance of programs and services required by part-time learners.**

6

Links Across and Within the Educational Spectrum

6.1 Preamble

One of the missions fundamental to the colleges' proposed renewed mandate is "to work together and with other educational institutions to offer students opportunities for educational mobility and lifelong learning."

Offering opportunities for educational mobility means, in practical terms, providing avenues for students to transfer from one type of institution to another; granting credit for prior learning and experience; and creating opportunities for educational and career advancement across the entire educational spectrum. In this chapter, we explore some of the ways to encourage these links. For Vision 2000, offering students an open educational horizon is an indispensable part of making our educational system ready for the 21st century.

6.2 System-Wide Evaluation of Prior Learning and Experience

Vision 2000 believes there should be an accessible and equitable system of evaluating the knowledge and skills people have acquired prior to their admission to a college program. There is a wide range of learning which should be taken into account — it may be from other educational institutions, in Ontario or in other jurisdictions, or it may be from on-the-job training or other non-institutional learning experiences. Formal recognition of students' previous learning and experience is one of the ways of putting lifelong learning into everyday practice.

Validating the educational achievements of individuals is akin to recognizing the value of an existing asset upon which new investments can be built. It encourages people to continue learning by giving them fair credit for what they have already learned. Determining the extent of an individual's educational achievement is important for individual learners, for educational institutions and for employers and organizations providing occupational or professional licensing.

For the individual, prior learning assessment should make a return to formal education a more attractive possibility. For many people, time spent away from the workforce to gain new knowledge and skills represents a high personal cost. Financial incentives, such as income support for training and paid educational leave, will influence the decisions people make. But such incentives cannot make up for the cost to individuals of having to repeat learning they have already attained because it is not recognized by the system.

The introduction of consistent and systematic prior learning assessment will help both individuals and organizations find a better fit. In the educational field, prior learning assessment is a crucial factor in granting admission and advanced standing; it also facilitates appropriate placement of students in programs and development of tailor-made study plans. For employers and organizations which provide occupational or professional licensing, fair, relatively inexpensive and accurate assessment is a critical part of making the right hiring decision and protecting the interests of the public.

Vision 2000 supports establishment of a system of universally accessible and equitable assessment of prior learning, which would provide the following benefits:

- encouraging enrolment by allowing the validation of a person's learning attainments to reduce both the amount of time and the redundant effort needed to acquire a formal educational credential;

- enhancing educational flexibility by opening up new possibilities for credit in different fields and from different sources, such as on-the-job experience or non-institutional training;

- improving the prospects of equal treatment of students seeking credit for prior learning by providing non-discriminatory, consistent and professional evaluations;

- providing a starting point for a full range of assessment services, including course/program placement and tailored educational counselling which assist student access to and completion of a course of study;

- helping colleges with the task of responding to the needs of employed workers by significantly improving the connections between the workplace and formal education;

- facilitating inter-institutional and inter-jurisdictional transferability by providing a means for assessing the equivalence of credits and academic achievement;

- reducing discrimination against groups, such as women re-entering the workforce and immigrants, whose achievements and experiences may be unfamiliar to employers and who may be unable to demonstrate their competence according to accepted standards;

- saving time and money for a wide range of institutions currently engaged in expensive and ad hoc efforts to assess prior learning;

- making prior learning assessment possible for those institutions which either found the effort prohibitively expensive or did not have the expertise to conduct proper assessments;

- guarding the public interest by ensuring that standards of competence are met, particularly in the realm of certified or licensed occupations, without turning away qualified individuals or forcing them to engage in unnecessary retraining; and

- offering an important avenue for faculty and staff at colleges and other public institutions to pursue lifelong learning by using their experience as a basis for further education.

Task Force on Access

The recent report of the Task Force on Access to Professions and Trades in Ontario[40] has provided a detailed analysis of the issues surrounding prior learning assessment. The report contains a careful consideration of how to define prior learning assessment and the progress being made in other jurisdictions in introducing workable policies. Although the primary focus of the Task Force was on access to professions and trades, particularly for those people with foreign credentials or experience, the analytical work and conclusions apply equally well in most instances to Ontario's educational institutions. Fortunately, the commissioners explicitly attempted to take into account the broader scope of prior learning assessment. As a result, there is a wealth of data and policy advice upon which to build.

The Task Force considered the two main dimensions of prior learning assessment: formal education and experiential learning.

Assessment of prior education: The Task Force found that in Ontario there are "recurring actual and potential weaknesses in the methods being applied to assess the educational backgrounds of applicants."[41]

The Task Force identified problems in the following areas: lack of recognition of academic qualifications, arbitrary standards, use of non-comprehensive outside evaluations, use of questionable international accrediting systems, unreliable reciprocity arrangements, complete lack of assessment of foreign training in certain cases, inconsistencies in the consideration of external factors, unjustified use of examinations to confirm equivalence, conflict-of-interest situations, overlapping jurisdictions, arbitrary requirements for registration in a prior jurisdiction of residency, rejection because of uncertainty, and lack of specificity and guidance in assessments.

Colleges are not immune to these problems. The Task Force found that all community colleges in Ontario appear to make some provision for or assessment of prior education, but that college assessment programs tend to be low profile and unsystematic. The Task Force notes that the "failure to assess [prior] education appropriately effectively negates an individual's ... accomplishments and results in either a complete rejection of prior education, by requiring the individual to repeat his or her entire training program here, or a requirement to complete partial retraining that may or may not be necessary. The result is frustration for the applicant and a waste of resources."[42]

---

[40] Task Force on Access to Professions and Trades in Ontario, *Access!* (Toronto: Ontario Ministry of Citizenship, 1989).

41 Ibid., p. 95.

[42] Ibid., pp. 99–100.

Assessment of prior experiential learning: Assessing prior experiential learning is a potentially significant avenue for awarding academic equivalence for a range of competencies acquired through actual on-the-job experience, structured employer-sponsored training, participation in volunteer activities or self-instruction.

However, as the Task Force points out, it is important to make sure that the standard against which the assessment of experiential learning is made must be the same as the one used in the assessment of prior academic learning. They argue strongly that the assessment of prior experience should take place on the basis of a "rigorous and detailed evaluation of learning achieved" and that the "assessment must focus on the competencies that the individual has actually acquired and not simply consider duration or contents of an individual's experience. In other words, it is the quality of learning, not the length of experience, that is relevant."[43]

While Ontario post-secondary institutions are beginning to address the challenge of assessing prior experience, the Task Force found that "recognition of experiential learning has not come easily to colleges and universities: our formal educational systems have evolved as bounded systems that do not happily acknowledge or attest to learning which they themselves have not initiated and regulated."[44] However, the Task Force said these institutions are beginning to recognize that valid and useful learning can take place in a variety of settings outside formal institutions. They found some evidence of case-by-case assessment of experiential learning in the colleges, but only rare instances where assessment of prior learning was formally recognized.

The Task Force also makes the point that efficient means for assessing experiential learning for academic credit and for occupational certification and licensing do exist. They discuss the experience of other jurisdictions which have systems in place.

Other Jurisdictions

Ontario is not alone in the drive to reach adult students, particularly from the world of work. The Task Force on Access points favourably to recent innovative efforts in other jurisdictions, particularly the United Kingdom, Quebec and British Columbia.

In the United Kingdom, the Credit Accumulation and Transfer Scheme (CAT) was established in 1984 by the Council for National Academic Awards. It is a mechanism for allowing people to graduate with course credits from different institutions and credits awarded for experiential learning. Students may receive credit for study in an industrial training centre or in a company's in-house education and training program. Each course unit is graded according to the quality of the performance at assessment; course units passed and grades earned are listed on a transcript. Both undergraduate and graduate degrees may be obtained by accumulating the appropriate credits. The Task Force notes: "This centrally administered CAT Scheme has created something very close to a

---

[43] Ibid., p. 103.

[44] Ibid., p. 103.

portable cumulative record of learning that brings academic and experiential learning together through a set of common standards and assessment strategies."[45]

Quebec introduced a strategy for comprehensive prior learning assessment in 1984 for its colleges of general and vocational education (CEGEPs). There were three elements to the strategy. First, the government established a provincial steering committee with a broad-based membership. This committee was given the task of setting out objectives as well as implementation, organizational and financial policies. The second step involved establishing a provincially funded technical assistance service to advise and support all levels of the prior learning assessment program. Finally, each college was asked to set up a prior learning assessment team composed of an administrator, an assessment counsellor, and specialized faculty advisers.

A review of the Quebec approach, contained in *The Barriers Project* report on obstacles to part-time learning, explains the objectives of the Quebec model as follows: "From the outset, the colleges have intended to implement a system of prior learning assessment which was credible (based on valid and reliable evaluations), comprehensive (utilizing different existing approaches), widely accessible and relatively inexpensive."[46]

British Columbia has combined prior learning assessment with a credit banking system. The B.C. Educational Credit Bank was established by provincial legislation within the B.C. Open Learning Agency. Students may be granted credit toward a degree, diploma or certificate through prior learning assessment. Credit may be based on skills and knowledge gained through a combination of independent study or travel, learning on the job, structured education and training not normally recognized for credit transfer, including education and training sponsored by employers and associations, and community volunteer work.

Prior Learning Assessment Network

It is time for Ontario to put prior learning assessment on a sound footing. Currently the obstacles are more at the level of institutional inertia and lack of will than in the realm of practical or functional precedents. Prior learning assessment can be done and is being done with relative success in other jurisdictions.

Looking at the needs of Ontario, the Task Force on Access recommends that an expert centralized body be established. The primary responsibility of this agency would be the assessment of prior academic and experiential learning and the designation of academic equivalence. The Task Force argues that a centralized approach is the most economical way to assemble the necessary resources and expertise and the best way to ensure quality of assessment. It notes that a central body would reduce duplication of effort by licensing bodies and educational institutions attempting individually

---

[45] Ibid., p. 123.

[46] Confederation College, *The Barriers Project* (Thunder Bay: Confederation College of Applied Arts and Technology, 1989).

to validate each applicant's prior education, and it would help to ensure consistency of treatment of individuals.

The Task Force elaborates a model of prior learning assessment which is aimed at resolving a number of challenges. One of their central concerns is that during the initial screening of applicants, the assessment of equivalence should be accessible, standardized and equitable. They describe the assessment of equivalence as the stage in the process that is "the most problematic, the most difficult, the least standardized, and the most open to abuse"[47] and they recommend the removal of this function to a specialized, systematized, and independent body.

Vision 2000 shares the concern that any mechanism for prior learning assessment must serve a broad constituency and offer fair, unbiased and professional service. We believe that the proposed Prior Learning Assessment Network (PLAN) can effectively serve the needs of Ontarians. We concur with the organizational premise of the PLAN proposal, which entails central co-ordination of decentralized assessment and information dissemination.

The Task Force outlines five characteristics of PLAN:

- it will have the power to delegate assessment procedures and administration;
- standards of competence must be developed through advisory committees which involve participation by the relevant body granting credentials;
- the representative advisory committees would assist assessors by providing advice on equivalence;
- there would be a general right to review assessments; and
- the agency must be run by an independent and fully representative board of directors.

The Task Force recommends an evolutionary approach which fits in well with the perspective adopted by Vision 2000. The PLAN is intended to have a three-year phase-in period during which the assessment procedures and standards would be established. Subsequently, the PLAN assessments, which are expected, more often than not, to be issued through a local assessment office, will be binding. This approach toward gradual and constituency-driven implementation is fully consistent with Vision 2000. Indeed, the concurrent emergence of PLAN, system-wide college program standards (through the College Standards and Accreditation Council [CSAC]) and the other co-ordinating and brokering bodies being proposed by Vision 2000 will greatly assist with the evolution of a learner-driven approach to lifelong learning.

 Recommendation 20

> **The government should establish the Prior Learning Assessment Network (PLAN), as recommended by the Task Force on Access to Professions and Trades in Ontario, with explicit inclusion of Ontario's colleges in the planning, implementation and operation of the system.**

---

[47] Ibid., p. 142.

6.3 Colleges and Schools

Historically, the schools and colleges have operated more or less in isolation from one another. While this has begun to change relatively recently, Vision 2000 believes that more needs to be done to break down the compartmentalization of the two systems. We looked at how co-ordination between secondary schools and colleges could be improved and increased while maintaining the integrity of the different institutional mandates.

We are convinced that the current and projected economic and social environment requires that a greater proportion of Ontario's population obtain further education and training beyond secondary school. Increasing the retention rate of secondary schools and assisting students' transition to further education will be necessary if we are to realize the goal of a better educated and more highly skilled labour force. Increasing the participation rate of secondary school graduates, as well as adults, in college programs will be necessary to reach such a goal.

If a greater number and proportion of secondary school students do not continue their education at the colleges, it is quite likely that their early work experiences will suggest the need for further education. As such, it appears to be a matter of when, rather than if, individuals choose to engage in further training. The large proportion of secondary school graduates who are qualified, but do not seek to further their education at the colleges, represents a considerable opportunity for the colleges to assist in the development of a more highly trained labour force.

Data for 1986 indicate that 32 per cent of Grade 9 students leave secondary school without a diploma.[48] Of those completing Grade 12, fewer than one in five (19.1 per cent) enrol directly in college programs. An additional nine per cent of graduates with a Secondary School Honours Graduation Diploma (i.e. Grade 13) enrol at a college. While registrations in apprenticeship programs have recovered from a slump in the mid-1980s (returning to 1981 levels), completion rates have declined.

One of the barriers to increasing the number and proportion of secondary school students engaged in post-secondary studies at the colleges is the apparent lack of information reaching students about the variety of college programs and the careers these lead to, and the opportunities for advanced training. Students must receive adequate information while they are in secondary school in order to make an informed choice about the future.

The limited information secondary school students receive about college programs may result in some choosing not to go to college or finding after graduation from high school school that they do not have the necessary prerequisites for admission to the college program of their choice. It may also reinforce a bias among some students toward university. In the next section, we discuss the

---

[48] Data cited in "Stimulating Statistics," February, 1990, Conference of the Association of Colleges of Applied Arts and Technology of Ontario.

---

relationship between colleges and universities and ways of enhancing opportunities for advanced training for college students.

Another barrier to success for many students is their lack of a sufficient academic background to succeed in their post-secondary programs. The attrition rate from college post-secondary programs — on average, more than 40 per cent — is similar to that of other jurisdictions, but it demonstrates that Ontario colleges have room for improvement. Though the underpreparedness of students leaving secondary schools is not the only factor contributing to attrition (students may leave college because they get a job, for example), academic difficulty is likely an important factor in a large number of cases. We have addressed the need for provision and funding of preparatory programming in the colleges in Chapter 5, but we believe that there should also be greater efforts at collaboration between the school and college systems to ease student transition from school to college.

Lack of collaboration between the school and college systems may be contributing to attrition rates in the secondary schools, as well as in the colleges. Some students, particularly at the general level, may leave high school before completing their diploma because they do not see any appealing career prospects ahead and they lack a clear perception of the occupational alternatives available to them and the means to reach them.

Our view is that efforts at retention at both the secondary school and college levels may benefit from a clearer and more consistent relationship between curriculum in the schools and the colleges. Joint school-college programs and earlier apprenticeship training are examples of initiatives which may provide attractive opportunities for youth to explore in their final years of secondary school and provide a focus for continued education.

Expanding school-college links

When the colleges were formed in the 1960s, the government announced its intention to bring school, college and university representatives together in a joint curriculum committee for each college. These committees, which were to investigate the ways in which programs of study at the different levels might be integrated, never materialized. In recent years, however, co-operative initiatives by local school boards and colleges have begun to develop and expand.

In 1989, the Ministries of Education and Colleges and Universities jointly released a blueprint for school-college links which encourages local collaboration and provides a general outline for the development and implementation of local "articulation" agreements. In 1990, the Ministry of Education (MOE) announced a $910,000 fund to further develop school-college links. In addition, a closer relationship between the two systems should be facilitated by MOE's initiative to establish core curricula through Grade 9, and to develop appropriate curricula for more specialized courses beginning in Grade 10.

Currently, there are examples of useful initiatives which demonstrate the potential benefits of greater co-operation between secondary schools and the colleges. Among the objectives these partnerships seek to achieve are:

- the development of complementary curricula, in specific subjects as well as services such as career counselling;
- the development of innovative ways to organize and deliver curriculum and services;
- the development of co-operative and mutually beneficial programs for human resource development of college and secondary school personnel; and
- the co-ordination and dissemination of information.

Vision 2000 supports the development of more and better partnerships between schools and colleges. We see potential for further development in several areas.

Clear and consistent program links between secondary schools and colleges should be developed to provide distinct paths to lifelong learning. Such paths appear particularly necessary to assist those secondary students at all levels who are uncertain about their occupational direction. By better linking secondary school and college curricula to provide more immediately accessible opportunities, we expect that more students would feel encouraged to explore options that the colleges can provide. The current initiative by MOE to develop new curriculum for the secondary schools offers an opportunity for co-operation. It is essential to involve college personnel in this process.

There are a number of directions for co-operative program delivery which may hold promise, such as combining secondary and post-secondary studies. For example, under a system which provides specialized offerings in senior secondary years, a student might embark on a four-year program starting with only high school courses, then introducing some college courses beginning in the second year, additional ones in the third year, and all college courses in the final year. Such a program might earn the student both a secondary school diploma as well as a college credential upon completion.

Another direction for co-operative delivery would combine school and work experiences. In addition to current co-op activities which provide credit for secondary school students, the School Workplace Apprenticeship Program has been established through a joint initiative of the Ministries of Education and Skills Development and involves a co-operative effort between a local school board, a college and local employers (for example, the Durham Board of Education, Durham College and a variety of Durham Region employers). The program provides a select group of students with an opportunity to learn both at school (high school and later at college) and on the job under the supervision of the Ministry of Skills Development. Upon completion, the students will have earned their secondary school diplomas as well as many hundreds of hours toward their apprenticeship.

Opportunities to combine employment and education should be encouraged. The proportion of secondary school leavers (dropouts and graduates alike) who are employed is significant, and colleges must treat such students as an important group whose needs can be better accommodated. Scheduling and funding changes to encourage part-time enrolment and a variety of program delivery options will be important to learners who are uncertain or apprehensive about undertaking further education.

There is considerable scope upon which to build co-operative activities in human resource development. For example, there appears to be a genuine need and desire on the part of some teaching staff at both colleges and secondary schools to further develop mutual appreciation and understanding. Co-operation might begin with more sharing of information on current programs and course options, as well as sharing of the data on students' needs and aspirations that are necessary for program planning. Such information might lead to co-operative career counselling activities, such as the North York Career Centre, which involves the North York Board of Education, Community Outreach and Education Foundation, COSTI-Education Centre, Employment and Immigration Canada, Jewish Vocational Services, York University and Seneca College; and the career counselling centres jointly funded by the City of Toronto, the Toronto Board of Education and George Brown College.

In addition, more focussed activities for joint professional development have been undertaken successfully and could be expanded. These have included, for example, an annual program involving Durham College, Durham Elementary Teachers Association and Ontario Secondary School Teachers Federation (District 17) in a program of workshops on a variety of topics. Similarly, a joint program of business education days involving the Mississauga Board of Trade, Peel Board of Education, Dufferin-Peel Separate School Board, Erindale College (of the University of Toronto) and Sheridan College has fostered information-sharing not only between educators from the different institutions, but with numerous local businesses as well.

Secondary school guidance counsellors are perceived by college personnel to be university-oriented, often lacking basic information about other opportunities. Given the breadth and diversity of college offerings, this is understandable; yet the colleges must assist the secondary school student to be better informed. To do so may require colleges to assist high school guidance personnel in reorienting career guidance to include more emphasis on non-university opportunities, not only for those not qualified for university, but also for the broad range of students considering university, colleges or direct entry into the labour force.

 Recommendation 21

> **The Ministry of Education, possibly through the newly formed Teacher Education Council of Ontario, should ensure that all teacher education programs (both pre-service and in-service) include components which furnish an in-depth knowledge of the educational services provided by the colleges. In particular, education about the colleges should be an explicit component of professional development for school guidance counsellors, teachers and principals.**

Vision 2000 is encouraged by the recent activity linking secondary schools and colleges at the local level. It is our view that the effectiveness of local arrangements will be enhanced by co-ordination between the secondary and college systems at the provincial level. This is particularly timely given that MOE is in the process of developing new curriculum guidelines for the secondary schools. Greater co-ordination at the provincial level is required to ensure that the momentum toward better school-college links is maintained and fostered at the local level, and to encourage more students to complete high school and to seek further educational opportunities at college.

 Recommendation 22

> **The Ministries of Education and Colleges and Universities should jointly establish a Provincial Schools/Colleges Co-ordinating Council, with representation of all relevant stakeholders from the secondary school and college systems, to improve school-college links and foster initiatives at the local level.**

The Council would perform the following functions:

- provide a forum for the co-ordination of curricula;

- facilitate the collaboration of schools and colleges in the development of new curricula;

- regularly publish a compendium of local "articulation" agreements and foster the development of innovative agreements (such as joint offerings);

- provide a framework for a co-ordinated communications effort aimed at giving students better and more accessible information concerning high school exit standards and college entrance standards; and

- develop strategies to encourage co-ordinated local (or regional) co-operative activities through local committees (or other administrative means) involving college and secondary school personnel.

Local co-ordinating committees could encourage colleges and local school boards to co-operate in expanding the number and scope of formal "articulation" agreements;[49] co-ordinating informal arrangements for laddering; developing co-operative professional development activities, such as teacher exchanges; and facilitating local strategies to improve student access and success.

Making the links work for high school students through effective provincial co-ordination is an important step. A further step, however, is to enable local colleges and school boards to assess needs and performance, undertake planning and evaluation, and adopt action plans. Simply establishing better links on paper is a necessary, but not a sufficient condition for achieving the goals of improved accessibility and higher success rates. Establishing local mechanisms for collaboration is an important next step toward realizing these goals.

By concentrating on the links between schools and colleges, this new Council is intended to assist students in realizing their educational aspirations across the entire spectrum of choices. The nature and scope of options available to learners depends upon schools and colleges working together with universities to expand and clarify Ontario's educational horizons.

---

[49] A discussion of alternative organizational models and examples of formal articulation agreements can be found in Jo Oppenheimer, "The Relationship Between Schools and Colleges," in *Colleges and the Educational Spectrum. Colleges and Schools. Background Papers* (Toronto: Ontario Council of Regents, 1989), pp. 60–66.

6.4 Colleges and Advanced Training Opportunities

In this section, we address two questions. First, is there a need to expand and improve the opportunities for college students and graduates to undertake more advanced training, some of which may be at the degree level? Second, if the need exists, how should it be met? By the term "advanced training" we mean education which combines the strong applied focus of college career-oriented programs with a strong foundation of theory and analytical skills.

College students now have limited access to advanced training through two routes: combining college with university studies, mainly through the provision of advanced standing in a university program, and some selected post-diploma offerings within the colleges. Ontario's colleges do not currently offer degree programs.

Current state of opportunities

Combining college with university studies: Enrolling in university programs represents one way college students and graduates may further their education at a more advanced level. In 1986-87, 3.4 per cent (1,362) of new registrants at Ontario's universities had attended college at some time.

Vision 2000 commissioned a survey of the colleges to determine what formal arrangements had been developed to facilitate college students' access to university programs.[50] The survey showed some increases in recent years in the numbers of arrangements. The responses revealed that, in total, 27 program-specific arrangements were operational, of which 23 were advanced standing (i.e. degree completion) arrangements and four involved the joint provision of a program by a college and a university. Of these 27 arrangements, 17 had been implemented since 1979; 11 of the 17 were implemented in 1988/89. Twelve colleges participated in these arrangements. Other arrangements are about to be implemented or are being negotiated which will bring the number of colleges involved to 14.

Typically, the arrangements are between one university and one college in a specific program area. However, there are a few universities (e.g. Lakehead and Laurentian) which have province-wide policies on credit for college courses in selected program areas. In early childhood education, two universities have developed arrangements with more than one college. Most of the program arrangements are in the liberal arts area or in areas that feed the service sector. Nearly half of all agreements are in three areas — early childhood education, business and general arts and science programs.

---

[50] Robert Alexander Marshall, "College-University Linkages in Ontario: Questionnaire Results," in *Colleges and the Educational Spectrum. Colleges and Universities. Background Papers* (Toronto: Ontario Council of Regents, 1989). In Marshall's survey, 19 of the 22 colleges responded. The Council of Ontario Universities has also collected data on college-university links which should be compared with Marshall's data.

Almost a third of the arrangements are with the University of Windsor. Another third of the arrangements involve universities in the United States. Two factors are important here: some colleges are located close to American universities, and American universities have a long tradition of college-to-university transfers.

In order to evaluate the impact of program-specific arrangements, the survey compared the credit given to college students under these arrangements with the general provisions for credit for college experience found in Ontario university calendars. In the absence of formal program-specific arrangements with a college, the maximum given to college students enrolling in university programs is five credits, or the equivalent of one year of university, provided they meet specific requirements. The survey found that, in general, college students received somewhat more credit where program-specific arrangements had been developed. The survey results also indicate that program-specific arrangements with American universities result in more credit for college courses than is the case with arrangements with Ontario's universities. (We have not examined evidence which would question the comparability of the American and Ontario university programs.)

Survey respondents indicated that a major reason for developing arrangements with a university is that they made college programs more attractive to potential students and were seen as a means of increasing enrolment in particular programs. Another reason frequently cited was that the arrangements were seen as a means of enabling each institution to contribute what it does best to the education and training of students.

Respondents noted that, on the whole, neither advanced standing nor joint program arrangements have led to, or required, significant changes in the nature of college programs. Some respondents noted some increase in emphasis being placed on analytic and communication skills. It appears that the further development of arrangements with universities could proceed without limiting the colleges' ability to serve those seeking the career-oriented training traditionally provided by colleges, although the more credit being sought, the more difficult it may be to maintain the distinctiveness of college programs.

The findings, although encouraging in some respects, point to some serious weaknesses in what might be termed the bilateral or laissez-faire model for developing college-university program arrangements. This approach has yielded rather limited and quite uneven opportunities for college graduates wanting to enrol in university programs in Ontario. Arrangements exist for only a limited number of programs, and there are very few arrangements in the technology fields. For the most part, arrangements for a particular program exist only at one or two colleges, and not at other colleges offering the program. In addition, when a college does negotiate an agreement, it is typically with only one university, causing extensive duplication of effort when the college seeks to extend such agreements.

Advanced training at the colleges: In selected program areas, such as the health sciences, colleges offer post-diploma studies. These studies are of short duration, typically one year or less, and the usual credential is a certificate. From the students' perspective, the lack of a well-recognized credential for post-diploma studies diminishes the status of these studies at colleges and may limit the investment students are willing to make in such courses and programs.

Pressures for improving opportunities

Although there may be some momentum developing in the area of college-university program arrangements, college students still have quite limited access to more advanced formal training. For many, a college diploma is perceived to be a terminal credential.

This can affect not only the future learning aspirations of qualified college graduates but also the enrolment decisions of new high school graduates contemplating post-secondary studies. The initial decision to attend college or university may be influenced by the student's knowledge that she or he will find it difficult to transfer from college to university with advanced standing. Some students, possibly ones who are better suited for college programs than university programs, may choose university over college because they conclude that it may not be feasible to attend university at a later date.

Meanwhile, the pressures to undertake more advanced training are increasing. In a number of fields of study, for example the health sciences, the training required, particularly in theory and technological applications, is increasing in both quantity and complexity. In addition, there is growing evidence that the North American economy requires some fundamental restructuring. Analyses undertaken by the Premier's Council (1988) in Ontario and the Massachusetts Institute of Technology's Commission on Industrial Productivity (1989) in the United States led these bodies to conclude that more emphasis must be placed on the development of high-value-added manufacturing industries which can compete in world markets.

In order for Ontario to undertake this restructuring, the supply of high-quality technologists and engineers will need to be increased. Compared with many other advanced economies, Ontario has relatively few engineers and technologists. The first report of the Premier's Council highlights some differences between Japan and Ontario. For example, in Japan there are 400 engineers per 10,000 workers, while in Ontario there are only 112; in contrast, for every 82 lawyers and accountants in Ontario, there are only four in Japan.

Through most of the 1980s the percentage of students enrolling in college technology and university engineering programs declined in Ontario. In addition, attrition in college technology programs is high, approaching 50 per cent. Many factors, including economic conditions in the manufacturing sector, have affected enrolment in these programs. It is likely, however, that changes will be necessary at all levels of education, from elementary school through university, in order to increase the supply of technologists and engineers.

Increasing the ability of students to move between the college and university sectors, in both directions, is one measure which should help increase the supply. Increasing the academic level of technology training in the colleges may be another positive measure.

The pace of technological change and the competitive pressures inherent in a global economy mean that individuals will be changing jobs and occupations much more frequently than in the past. (Current estimates in the U.S. are that those now entering the labour force will have, on average, slightly more than six different jobs over the course of their working life.) College graduates, therefore, will need to be assured that their training provides a good foundation for lifelong learning and that it will be appropriately recognized if, at some stage, their career aspirations lead them to seek further formal education at a higher level.

The practice of credentialism by employers — "the practice of selecting individuals for entry to certain job fields, or advancement within those fields, on the basis of their formal educational qualifications even though the specific content of their education may not be absolutely required for the performance of the tasks involved in their jobs"[51] — means that some competent college graduates are dead-ended in their careers.

Those who have examined the issue of credentialism have concluded that this practice may represent, in economic terms, rational behaviour on the part of employers, and thus may be difficult to change. On average, performance may be correlated with the level of individuals' educational credentials, making credentials a cost-effective screening device for employers. However, basing hiring decisions on credentials will, at the same time, result in the unequal treatment of equally productive individuals. This practice results in the underutilization of the talents of individuals.

The practice of credentialism is not limited to employers. In the fields of nursing, physiotherapy and industrial accounting, for example, professional associations are attempting to make a degree a prerequisite for entry into practice. Others may follow, in such fields as child care, early childhood education and other social services. The motivation for instituting degree requirements may be to ensure that the practitioners are of high quality or to enhance the stature and bargaining power of those in the profession. To the extent that it is the former, it may be in the public interest to enhance the training provided in these fields. To the extent it is the latter, such professional self-interest may need to be regulated.

It must also be stressed that even if our economy's structure were not expected to change, adherence to the principle of equitable access would require improvements in advanced training opportunities for college students and graduates. At present, almost 85 per cent of college post-secondary students enrol at age 24 or younger. An educational or career decision made at this relatively young age should not limit the opportunities to embark upon other educational or career paths. But unless it is possible to receive an appropriate amount of credit for courses taken at a college and for relevant work experience, the doors to university studies will effectively remain closed for many people.

Many of the pressures affecting college-bound students and college graduates will also affect university students. The expected increased need for applied training should result in greater numbers of university students seeking college courses. It is as important, therefore, to ensure that

---

51 Ibid., p. 2.

these students receive fair credit for their university work when moving into college programs. The demand for entry into college programs by university students is already significant. In 1986/87, 5.2 per cent of the 95,000 full-time post-secondary students in the colleges had some previous university experience, and an additional 1.7 per cent were university graduates.

Implications for the future

As identifiable as the pressures for advanced training appear to be, forecasting the number of individuals who would or should avail themselves of such opportunities is very difficult; and the specific programs in which the need for more advanced training will be greatest is uncertain. Further, there is no consensus about the educational implications of, for example, restructuring Ontario's economy. Some believe that one appropriate focus would be an expansion of degree-level polytechnic education in engineering and technology programs; others contend that the larger need will be for more and better students at the diploma level, in the technician-technologist area. At the same time, still others argue that the aging of our population and the increasing cultural diversity of the population require a more balanced approach to the expansion of opportunities; that is, as much attention should be paid to the health science and social service fields as to the engineering/technology fields.

The pressures outlined above are important not only because of their implications for the expansion of advanced training opportunities in general; they also raise questions about the appropriate distribution of these opportunities between the college and university sectors. In considering a particular advanced training need, it will be necessary to determine whether the need would be most effectively addressed by a program offered through a college, a university, a collaborative venture, or some new approach.

Over the past several decades, there has been an expansion in the number and types of degree-level programs offered by Ontario's universities. Many of these programs are quite occupation-specific. Some examples include programs in education, journalism and computer science. Often the programs have been developed in response to emerging occupational fields (e.g. computer science or environmental studies), or in response to significant changes in knowledge and skill requirements within a traditional occupational field (e.g. education). In addition, a desire by some occupational groups (e.g. chartered accountants) to raise their earnings and status within the occupational hierarchy has, in some instances, contributed to the requirement that practitioners possess a degree, although not necessarily a degree specifically related to the occupational field.

If this expansionary tendency continues, and we expect it will, there may be major consequences for both the college and university sectors in Ontario. There may be more pressures to develop programs of more advanced training in areas which have been mainly the responsibility of the college system. To date, when such pressures have developed and led to degree programs, it has been the university sector which has assumed responsibility for these programs, with the college sector in some instances (e.g. physiotherapy) more or less relinquishing its role in providing training in these fields.

At some stage, however, the university sector may not be receptive to further expansion of its degree offerings, particularly in fields which have not as yet attained professional status but are attempting to do so. In addition, the university sector may resist major expansions in some of its existing occupation-specific degree programs. Such programs, when offered on a relatively small scale, may not be viewed as adversely altering the universities' mandate and image. However, major expansions in university enrolment, in a field such as nursing in which there are 9,300 students enrolled in the college system, might be viewed as intruding on the more traditional roles in education and research of Ontario's universities.[52]

The universities already face physical capacity constraints. This problem would be compounded if, for example, in the health sector an increasing proportion of nurses and other health practitioners were required to undertake degree-level training, as some in the field are proposing, and this training took place only at the universities. The pressures on university space would become particularly acute if, as many expect, there is rapid growth in demand for health care as a result of the aging population and continued advances in medical technologies.

In reviewing the past and looking to the future, we conclude that it will continue to be in the public interest to elevate the rigour and broaden the comprehensiveness of selected programs of study and to develop advanced programs for selected emerging occupations. It is important, therefore, to consider not only the appropriate institutional location (college or university) but also the appropriate credential.

In the present context, the assumption has been that programs of advanced training must offer degrees in order to attract competent students. As much as we may disapprove of the importance that we as a society attach to credential titles, the fact remains that an individual's employment, status and earnings are affected by credential titles. The degree has been and is likely to remain the pre-eminent credential.

In the future, if the colleges are to play an effective role in providing a range of career-oriented advanced training opportunities, a unique college credential will be required. Whatever the credential — a degree or some other designation — it must be one which reflects the rigour, comprehensiveness and occupational focus of new programs aimed at meeting emerging needs.

Strategic directions

Expansion of advanced training opportunities presents a difficult educational policy problem. On the one hand, strong impressionistic evidence suggests that there is a need to improve the opportunities for more advanced training for college students and graduates; on the other hand, there is uncertainty about the size and nature of the specific needs.

---

[52] A discussion of these issues in the context of nursing education is found in Michael L. Skolnik, *Some Unthinkable Options for Implementing the Entry to Practice Proposal for Nursing in Ontario — A View from Outside the Profession* (unpublished paper, 1988).

In the foreseeable future, improved co-ordination and more effective utilization of existing resources in the two post-secondary sectors should be sufficient to provide the necessary expansion of opportunities for college students and graduates seeking access to more advanced institutional training and education. At this time, therefore, we do not recommend building, in a physical sense, new post-secondary institutes such as polytechnics or a university of applied arts and technology.

Nor would it be desirable to undertake a wholesale transformation of selected colleges into institutions dedicated to higher-level training. Such a decision would harm the status of those colleges which did not receive this designation; the consequences could be serious if the result were that fewer students decided to attend colleges.

To meet the need for more advanced training, we propose that efforts be directed toward expanding opportunities for combining college and university studies, and for higher-level training within the colleges themselves.

We believe that these directions will result in a post-secondary system in Ontario in which the college and university sectors more effectively complement each other. The related recommendations in this section are designed to ensure that the college and university sectors retain distinctive — but equally important — roles, each doing what it does best, while at the same time increasing the opportunities for college and university students to move between the two sectors.

In a post-secondary system in which the two sectors are linked horizontally, students' decisions about whether to attend college or university will not be constrained by a concern that choosing one route will effectively close the doors to the other. A more "permeable" post-secondary system will help provide a distribution of students between colleges and universities which primarily reflects lifelong learning needs, rather than institutional rigidities.

Recommendation 23
The Minister of Colleges and Universities should endeavour to expand and improve the opportunities for students to move between the college and university sectors, while maintaining the distinctiveness of each sector.

In defining improved opportunities, we establish the goal that students, whatever their college and whatever their post-secondary program area, should have opportunities, limited only by their geographic mobility, to undertake degree studies at a university which take into account their college experience in a fair manner.

Achieving this goal would mean, for example, that students of similar achievement levels enrolled in business programs with similar objectives at colleges A and B would receive the same amount of credit upon entry to University X's degree program in commerce. These students would also receive the same amount of credit as provided by University X if enrolling in a comparable program at University Y.

In part, achieving this goal will depend on the development of consistent program standards across the college system. Universities are reluctant to grant credit for academic work over which they cannot guarantee the quality. Undertaking a concerted effort to establish and ensure college system standards and to broaden curriculum, as proposed in earlier recommendations, should considerably diminish these concerns.

Consistent with improved opportunities is the provision of combined college-university studies in a variety of formats. As is current practice in Ontario's post-secondary system, opportunities should be structured in a variety of ways, depending on the nature of the students and programs, including:

- **advanced standing arrangements in related fields of study:** For example, a college business graduate would be granted advanced standing in a university commerce program and after completing selected courses at a university would receive a B.Comm.; or a college general arts and science graduate could be granted advanced standing in a university arts or science program, leading to a B.A. or B.Sc.

- **general transfer credits for students moving between unrelated fields of study:** For example, a college business student would be granted advanced standing in a university social work program and after completing selected courses at a university would receive a B.S.W.

- **custom degree-completion programs for college graduates at universities:** College graduates, with their own course sections, complete degree programs; two examples of programs customized for college graduates are Lakehead's engineering program and Ryerson's child and youth care program.

- **joint program offerings by colleges and universities:** A student would concurrently take university and college courses and upon successful completion receive a college diploma and university degree.

- **diploma-completion arrangements:** A university student or graduate would be granted advanced standing in college diploma programs.

In developing program-specific arrangements with universities, colleges should ensure that they do not alter their programs in a manner which would be inconsistent with their primary mandate — the provision of career-oriented education at the certificate and diploma levels. Although placing this restriction on the development of arrangements with universities may limit somewhat the amount of credit universities will be able to award students for college experience, it is crucial that college post-secondary programs continue to meet the needs of those learners who do not have university aspirations or abilities.

In a related context, the question has been asked whether Ontario's colleges should have university transfer programs. Such programs might be two years long, in general arts and science, and would be composed of university-equivalent courses. Following successful completion, students would be able to enter directly into the third year of a comparable program at a university. These types of programs are available in other jurisdictions. In some instances, as in British Columbia, a significant motivation for placing such programs in colleges has been that access to university is constrained by geographical distances. This does not appear to be a significant problem in Ontario. For some, another argument in favour of these transfer programs is that the academic courses in these programs would have a positive effect on the "scholarly ethos" of colleges. We remain concerned, however, that these programs might detract from the career-oriented educational role of colleges. It is our conclusion, and that of the majority of stakeholders with whom we consulted, that such traditional transfer programs should not become part of the colleges' program offerings at this time.

In addition to improving opportunities for college students to obtain advanced training at a university, we believe that, in some instances, the colleges themselves should provide advanced training. This may be particularly appropriate in emerging occupational fields including some of those dependent on new technologies. The colleges' vocational orientation, their relations with employers, and the practical work experience of many of their faculty would all contribute to the effective provision of such programs. Among good candidates for the college sector would be applied fields of study, requiring strong theoretical foundations, for which there are clear benefits to combining learning in classrooms and libraries with learning in the workplace itself.

Examples of suitable programs might include manufacturing systems engineering, digital systems engineering, nursing, early childhood education, graphic design and fashion. Some programs might be offered in partnership with business and industry. For example, programs might be structured in a "sandwich mode," alternating periods of institutional instruction with related work placement. Instruction from regular college faculty might also be augmented by some classroom instruction from experts in business and industry, who have been provided release time by their employers. Such partnerships would signal employers' commitment to a particular program, as well as enhancing program quality.

In some instances it may be appropriate for colleges to share resources in providing these programs. For example, the first two years of an advanced program might be offered at selected colleges across the system, with the latter stages of the program being provided at only one or two of these colleges. With this approach, a critical mass of faculty, equipment and students is ensured as students move into the final and more specialized year(s) of their program.

Credit transfer arrangements would need to be developed to facilitate the movement of students enrolled in regular college programs or in university programs into these advanced programs. The advanced programs, focussing on the application of knowledge and skills in the workplace, would be more vocationally oriented than traditional university arts and science programs. As such, they would complement existing college diploma programs, thus providing, we believe, reasonable scope for awarding credit to college students transferring into them.

 Recommendation 24

> **The college system should develop comprehensive programs of advanced training, on a selective basis, to address student needs. Graduates of such programs should receive a unique credential at the post-diploma level.**

Students graduating from these programs should be awarded a distinctive credential at the post-diploma level, possibly a provincial credential. Many consider that a degree would be the appropriate credential, given that attempts to establish an alternative credential which confers comparable status and earning power have been unsuccessful. This has been a long-standing concern. For example, recognizing the need for "tangible symbols of accomplishment," the Commission on Post-Secondary Education in Ontario recommended in 1972 that colleges "be permitted, if they wish to award distinctive bachelors' degrees, such as the Bachelor of Technology and the Bachelor of Applied Arts ..."[53] However, as was the case in the 1970s, there may be obstacles in today's environment to offering a degree for college-based programs of advanced training. In addition to the historical reluctance of the provincial government to extend degree-granting authority beyond publicly-funded universities, the university sector has expressed concerns about the possible impact of expanding the number and types of degrees.

Our immediate goal is that the college system (and the provincial government) be able to respond to the pressures we have identified by expanding opportunities for advanced training. It is our judgment that, at this juncture, efforts to resolve the issue of what is the appropriate credential would merely detract from the overriding objective of designing and mounting appropriate programs.

A provincial institute without walls

Vision 2000 proposes a mechanism to implement the preceding strategic directions: providing increased opportunities for college students to undertake university studies and to pursue advanced training at the colleges.

To achieve the necessary expansion and improvement in arrangements for combined college-university studies, we propose the establishment of a provincial institute. It would not only facilitate and co-ordinate the development of arrangements between colleges and universities but would also offer programs of combined studies. In addition, it would be involved in the development of college-based programs of advanced training.

 Recommendation 25

> The government should establish a provincial institute "without walls" for advanced training to:
> - **facilitate the development and co-ordination of arrangements between colleges and universities for combined college-university studies;**
> - **offer combined college-university degree programs, with instruction based at and provided by colleges and universities; and**
> - **recommend, where appropriate, to the College Standards and Accreditation Council the development of college-based programs of advanced training with a unique credential at the post-diploma level.**

An institute with these three functions will have a range of options for providing advanced training opportunities which involve using existing instructional resources, including space, in our post-secondary system.

Function 1: The Institute will act as a co-ordinating body, providing leadership in the development of college-university links. It will endeavour to facilitate the development of program-specific and curriculum-specific arrangements between colleges and universities in the formats

---

[53] Commission on Post-Secondary Education in Ontario, *The Learning Society* (Toronto: Ministry of Government Services, 1972), pp. 49-50.

discussed earlier. The credentials awarded for successful completion of these combined college-university studies will be those of the colleges and universities which the students attend.

If there is reluctance among some colleges and universities to engage in the development of college-university links, the Institute might encourage the development of a consortium or consortia of colleges and universities with reasonably common objectives, which would undertake to develop arrangements. To initiate this approach, the Institute could establish some principles on which arrangements should be based and then ask which colleges and universities want to participate.

The Institute should publish annually a calendar which describes the arrangements reached between colleges and universities and the Institute's programs of combined college-university studies.

Function 2: The Institute will offer programs which combine college and university courses. The required courses will be drawn mainly from existing course offerings at the universities and colleges; and the programs will be structured in both sequential (degree-completion) and concurrent forms. Instruction will take place at the colleges and universities, and these institutions will grade the students' performance. The Institute will provide funding to the colleges and universities for the provision of these instructional services. Its board will be responsible for determining the programs' admission requirements, the criteria for advanced standing, the required courses and the exit standards.

This second function is important from at least three perspectives. First, it may result in the development of more innovative and flexible combinations of college and university courses than those possible in the existing arrangements between colleges and universities. Second, the Institute, being less bound by tradition than existing institutions, may become a leader in assessing applicants' prior learning and experience. However, developing the appropriate assessment criteria and techniques are major tasks. The Institute should therefore work in conjunction with any agencies that, as a result of the recommendations of the Task Force on Access to Professions and Trades in Ontario (1989), are given responsibility for developing assessment mechanisms. And third, where it has not been possible for universities and colleges to establish agreements in program areas for which there are identifiable needs for combined college-university studies, the Institute, through offering these combined studies programs, will be able to meet these needs.

 Recommendation 26

> **A formal agreement of association between the Institute and one or more Ontario universities should be established, providing for the associated universities to grant their degrees to graduates of programs conducted under the auspices of the Institute.**

We believe that it is desirable for programs conducted under the auspices of the Institute to have credentials offered through an existing degree-granting institution. In the long run, the value of the Institute's programs will be a function of the esteem in which their graduates are held; but in the immediate future, the Institute's programs and graduates would have more immediate credibility through an association with an existing university.

Of necessity, such an association would need to provide for the degree-granting institution to issue degrees, at the direction of the Institute, for a range of combined college-university studies, many of which may not have involved instruction at the granting institution. For example, in an association between the Institute and University X, students engaged in an Institute program involving technology studies at College Y and engineering courses at University Z would receive their B.Eng. from University X. While we recognize that this requirement will make such an agreement of association difficult to achieve, we believe several Ontario universities will give serious consideration to this creative venture in outreach and access.

Given the importance of providing college students and graduates fair and consistent access to university-level education, a firm date for completion of an agreement must be established. We therefore propose that a committee, composed of representatives of the Ministry of Colleges and Universities (MCU), the Council of Regents, the Ontario Council on University Affairs, the Council of Presidents, and the Council of Ontario Universities (under the direction of the Deputy Minister of MCU), be established to facilitate an agreement of association.

 Recommendation 27

> **In the event that an agreement of association between the Institute and one or more universities cannot be reached within eighteen months, the government should vest degree-granting authority in the Institute itself.**

If degree-granting authority were vested in the Institute, its role would be similar to that of the Council for National Academic Awards (CNAA) in the United Kingdom, for example, under whose auspices degree programs are offered by polytechnics. Through rigorous examination of degree submissions and of the staff and facilities of polytechnics proposing to offer degree programs, this body has been able to ensure the quality and market value of its polytechnic degree programs. In addition, as noted in section 6.2, the CNAA has established the Credit Accumulation and Transfer Scheme, which allows students to obtain credentials by combining credits from different institutions.

In whatever form the Institute's programs are established, it will be necessary for the Institute to reach agreement with universities and colleges for the admission of Institute students to their courses. Current provisions at colleges and universities for admission of special students may need to be augmented. Further, the Institute's resources should be sufficient to allow it to provide the universities and colleges with funding equivalent to their respective per-student grants. This would reduce the likelihood that the admission of Institute students would result in other students being denied access to the college or university courses.

Function 3: The Institute's third function, that of recommending to CSAC the development of college-based programs of advanced training, is a natural by-product of its first two functions.

As part of its work in relation to the first two functions, the Institute will initiate analyses and undertake consultations with industrial/occupational sectors to determine the program areas in which the need for advanced training is greatest. The analyses should include a determination of the nature and level of the required training in order for the Institute to decide the appropriate venue(s) for a given program. These studies would be conducted in conjunction with CSAC's program councils.

Without specific sectoral studies and without, for example, a clear sense of the industries which the provincial and federal governments intend to promote, the Institute will be hard pressed to determine the advanced training initiatives to which it should give priority. In stressing the importance of undertaking these sectoral-specific analyses, we note past experiences surrounding the issue of expansion of polytechnic education in Ontario. This issue has received sporadic attention since at least 1980, when the Ontario MCU commissioned a study on polytechnic education in England and Wales, and issued a discussion paper entitled *Polytechnic Education in Ontario*. Definitive conclusions were not reached and are unlikely to be reached through further abstract, macro-level research.

Where need is demonstrated, the Institute will assess the alternative ways for meeting this need — university-based degree programs, combined college-university studies, or college-based advanced training programs. If, as a result of the Institute's assessment, a college-based program is determined to be the best option, it will recommend to CSAC that it give consideration to initiating the development of the program. In turn, CSAC might seek program proposals from interested colleges and, where appropriate, request a college or colleges to mount the program.

Membership of the Institute board: Given the Institute's range of functions and the importance of developing partnerships in order to effectively undertake these functions, its board should include representatives from the colleges, the universities, business and industry, labour and government. Representation from the colleges and universities should include students (or alumni), faculty and administrators. The distribution of representation might be 40 per cent from the colleges, 40 per cent from the universities, and 20 per cent from business, labour and government. If an agreement of association with a university (or consortium) is reached, representatives from that university should constitute a significant proportion of overall university representation.

For an institute of this type to have a significant and lasting impact on advanced training opportunities for college students and graduates, it will need to produce results which are demonstrably good. Although there are no guarantees and much of what the Institute undertakes in its initial years will need to be viewed as experimental, the Institute will be well positioned to undertake these new initiatives. It will not need to concern itself with many of the day-to-day operational problems faced by other educational institutions — the Institute will require neither a large physical plant nor large numbers of staff. The Institute will be able to focus its resources on the co-ordination and development of advanced training opportunities, on criteria for admission and advanced standing, and on the monitoring of its students' progress while in school and after graduation. In short, it will be relatively specialized in the issues and problems which it addresses, and the quality of its performance should reflect this clearly defined focus.

7

Working as a System

7.1 Preamble

Vision 2000 has pointed out the importance of colleges increasing their links and partnerships with other educators and with the community. We have also urged the colleges to "work as a system" in order to tackle some of the pressing challenges in the years ahead.

All institutions strive for greater effectiveness in realizing organizational goals. In times of fiscal restraint, planning and collaborative decision-making are particularly crucial if important objectives are to be achieved without sacrificing institutional integrity. We anticipate public funds will continue to be limited, and colleges will need to find ways to do more than cope. Therefore, it will be important for colleges to work together to meet the challenges of the future.

One of the major questions facing colleges is how the system should respond to the conflicts or trade-offs between quality, access and funding. The resolution of these conflicts and the process by which that resolution is arrived at ultimately determines the performance of the college system. The resolution of these conflicts also affects how the system is perceived by learners, their families, those who work in the colleges, employers and taxpayers at large. It is essential, therefore, that colleges address the trade-offs, and it is by working as a system that they will develop the most effective solutions.

One important way of working as a system is through sharing resources. This can be accomplished in a variety of ways, for instance by sharing specialized resources through partnerships. A college known for its expertise in a particular field can share its faculty and materials with other colleges, making the entire system more effective and increasing accessibility. Another way of sharing resources is by joining forces to tackle some fundamental issue that affects the entire system. This may involve using information, data and the participation of the entire system to develop strategic responses.

7.2 What are the Quality-Access-Funding Trade-Offs?

The interrelationships between quality, access (in terms of both numbers and types of students) and funding are not easily defined. Nor are the trade-offs inherent in these relationships easily measured.

One of the reasons it is difficult to ascertain the impact of funding on quality and access is that the effects may not be evident immediately. For example, if the total revenue of the college system, measured in constant dollars, remains fixed over a given period of time, it may be possible initially to increase enrolment without lowering the quality of instruction. Colleges can accommodate the increased enrolment by reducing expenditures on equipment, capital maintenance and professional development of staff; by reducing program hours (with commensurate increases in independent study); and by increasing the utilization of their staff.

In the short run, these adjustments may lead to increased access through gains in efficiency: reductions in per-student expenditures without accompanying reductions in quality. And some measures, such as improved utilization of staff and facilities, may even provide permanent efficiency gains.

In the long run, however, continuing this funding policy could lead to other consequences. Equipment will not deteriorate overnight, nor will staff performance. This can lead to a false sense of security among government and college decision-makers. It may also lead to following a particular policy direction — in this example, increasing access without increasing real revenues — to the point that unintended outcomes occur, such as unacceptable reductions in quality.

It is the long-term consequences of these trade-offs, not always immediately evident, that must concern the government and the college system. In order to achieve many of the directions outlined by Vision 2000, the system must gain a better understanding of the nature of the trade-offs between quality, access and funding.

7.3 Effects of the Trade-Offs, 1978/79 to 1988/89

In this section we examine the trade-offs between quality, access, and funding over the period 1978/79 to 1988/89 in relation to college activity funded by the Ministry of College and Universities (MCU). Activity supported by MCU accounts for the majority of the college system's revenues, more than 60 per cent when one takes into account the associated tuition revenues. These activities, mainly full-time post-secondary programs, have largely been under the control of the colleges; the colleges have determined the number of students to admit, initiated proposals for new programs to be approved by MCU and, to a large degree, they have been responsible for program standards. Other training activities of the colleges, such as skills training programs sponsored by the Ontario Ministry of Skills Development (MSD) and Canada Employment and Immigration Commission (CEIC), are also subject to quality-access-funding trade-offs. However, the objectives of the programs and access to them are the result of specific decisions by the sponsoring agencies. Given these differences and the availability of consistent time-series data on MCU-funded activity, the discussion in this section is limited to programs supported by MCU.

The funding process itself requires a brief description. The operating funds provided to each college by MCU are the result of a two-stage process. First, the Ministry "negotiates" an allocation for the college system from the provincial Treasury. The Ministry then distributes this allocation among the colleges through an activity-based distribution mechanism, often referred to as the funding formula.

The mechanism calculates activity based on weighted enrolments. The weighting factors reflect differences in unit costs among programs and differences among colleges in characteristics, such as geography and size, which affect the costs of providing access to an appropriate range of programs. A college's share of the system's overall operating grant is based on its share of system activity in the period two and three years earlier. For example, a college's share of the 1989/90 operating grant is equal to the sum of its activity in 1986/87 and 1987/88 divided by the total activity of the system in these two years.

With this method of funding, it is important to recognize that the government does not announce a level of funding per student. Rather, it announces each college's operating grant, and only after enrolment is known for that funding year can the level of funding per student be calculated. Thus, from the government's perspective, funding is not open-ended, as it would be if the government established a level of funding per student and agreed to provide this level, whatever the system's total enrolment.

During the period 1978/79 to 1983/84, the total MCU operating grant, measured in constant dollars, increased 1 per cent. Over the same period, enrolment increased 49 per cent; therefore, real funding per student provided to colleges by MCU declined approximately 33 per cent.

What happened to the colleges during this time period could be interpreted in a number of ways. One could see the statistics as indicating a dramatic increase in efficiency, with no offsetting declines in quality; or one could conclude that there was a decline in quality; or the numbers could be read as showing some combination of an increase in efficiency and a decrease in the quality of education. Data provided at the time were interpreted by government to suggest that real gains in efficiency were being made.[54] However, that interpretation was challenged by college faculty and subsequently in

---

[54] See Report of Task Force on Productivity Indices, *An Analysis of Unit Operating Costs in Ontario's Colleges of Applied Arts and Technology, 1978-79 to 1982-83* (Toronto: Ministry of Colleges and Universities, 1984).

the report of the Instructional Assignment Review Committee (IARC), which examined issues relating to faculty workload following the faculty strike in 1984.[55]

In part, this decline in real funding per student was of the colleges' own making. They resisted managing enrolment in a manner which would have lessened the impact of declines in aggregate funding on per-student funding levels. One can probably attribute their resistance in large part to three factors, namely:

- a strong commitment to maximizing accessibility;

- problems of measurement — the number of qualified applicants being turned away can be measured, but measuring quality (and the impacts of different levels of quality) is considerably more difficult and subject to a variety of interpretations. As a result, public awareness of the effects on accessibility of decisions by colleges (and government) tends to make decision-makers responsive to accessibility concerns; and

- the activity-based funding distribution mechanism, which may cause colleges to increase their enrolment beyond reasonable limits in an effort to increase or at least maintain revenues.

Between 1983/84 and 1988/89 the funding per student increased, although it did not return to the level achieved in the late 1970s. Over this five-year period, the total MCU operating grant, measured in constant dollars, increased 22 per cent. However, enrolment remained essentially unchanged, increasing only 1 per cent. The result was that real funding per student increased approximately 21 per cent.

The low enrolment growth over this period was not the result of limiting access — there is no evidence that applicants were being turned away. Instead, enrolment rates in the colleges may have been affected by improving economic conditions and reaction to concerns about the quality of college education expressed during the faculty strike.

Some other important changes were also taking place during this period. Contract negotiations, which followed the report of IARC, resulted in significantly reduced teaching hours for faculty. To maintain accessibility under the contractually defined reductions in workload, $60 million was provided to allow for the hiring of additional faculty (approximately 800, an increase of 11 per cent).

What happened within the colleges during the period 1983/84 to 1988/89 may also be interpreted in a number of ways. Efficiency in providing educational services may have declined; or the quality of instruction may have increased; or some combination of the two may have occurred. Again, it is a matter of interpretation, in the current absence of agreed-upon indicators.

---

[55] See Report of the Instructional Assignment Review Committee, *Survival or Excellence?* (Toronto: Ministry of Colleges and Universities, 1985).

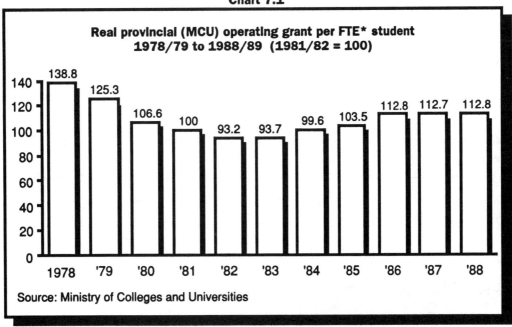

Chart 7.1

**Real provincial (MCU) operating grant per FTE* student
1978/79 to 1988/89 (1981/82 = 100)**

Source: Ministry of Colleges and Universities

*Full-time equivalent

It should also be pointed out that during this period the colleges faced new demands which resulted in increased operating costs, some of which were the result of new government initiatives. For example, the Freedom of Information Act and pay equity legislation placed additional cost pressures on the colleges. More recently, the payroll tax to support the Ontario Health Insurance Plan and the costs resulting from the settlement of support staff and faculty contracts after the 1989 faculty strike have further contributed to cost pressures.

In addition to the pattern of per-student funding we have described, there have been significant variations in grant increases — both within a given year among colleges and from one year to the next at individual colleges. In each of the years from 1981/82 to 1989/90, the difference in grant increase between the colleges receiving the lowest and highest increases exceeded 10 percentage points. With respect to year-to-year variations for individual colleges, grant increases varied, for example, in the period 1981/82 to 1983/84 from 12.1 per cent to 5.7 per cent (Fanshawe); and from 5.1 per cent to 15.8 per cent (Loyalist). In this period the system's operating grant allocation increased about 11.5 per cent each year.

The range of grant increases reflects differences in the historical rates of enrolment growth among the colleges, and therefore may be seen to represent an equitable distribution of operating funds. The magnitude of the variance, however, may be a source of some concern — both to the extent to which it reflects counter-productive enrolment growth[56] and to the extent to which the working environment within individual colleges is adversely affected.

---

[56] We can describe growth as counter-productive if it represents an attempt on the part of a college to maintain or enhance its share of the system's operating grant without sufficient regard to either the effects on the quality of programs or the need for growth in particular program areas.

In summary, the funding policies of government and the manner in which colleges responded to funding restraints have contributed to unintended outcomes. Two of the most notable outcomes have been the discontent among college faculty, which led to a strike in 1984, visibly demonstrating the divergent views of labour and management on educational issues; and the perception, held by many people, that the quality of college education declined, particularly before the implementation of the new faculty workload agreement in 1986.

The events of the past decade also have revealed that effective mechanisms or processes are not in place for either examining the quality-access-funding relationships or determining which actions are likely to be most effective in minimizing the negative effects and unintended outcomes of the trade-offs inherent in these relationships. There does appear to be consensus within the system, however, that changes to the structure of funding may represent one effective course of action.

7.4 How to Deal with the Trade-Offs in the Future

Over the next two decades, Ontario will experience a dramatic aging in its population, accompanied by significant economic, technological and demographic change (e.g. low birth rate, a larger multicultural population). These forces are expected to put new demands on all areas of public expenditure, including increased pressure for access to post-secondary education.

The result is that colleges can anticipate an increasing demand for places in the system at a time when government resources are limited. For the government and the system, the challenge is to meet this demand while maintaining or improving quality. Anticipating these conditions, Vision 2000, asks: how can *unintended* outcomes, such as poor-quality education, be avoided, and how can *undesirable* outcomes, such as reduced access, be minimized?

A College System Strategic Planning Committee

The task of analyzing the impacts of the quality-access-funding trade-offs needs to be part of a broader strategic planning process which includes a quality-sensitive component. Vision 2000 believes that to better understand and cope with the quality-access-funding relationships in the future, the colleges must work as a unit — pooling the knowledge, resources and analytical abilities within the individual colleges to develop strategic, system-wide responses to the trade-offs.

 Recommendation 28

A College System Strategic Planning Committee should be established by the Council of Regents. This standing committee would:
- undertake research on the quality-access-funding trade-offs facing Ontario's colleges;
- disseminate analyses and information across the college system; and
- recommend strategies to the Minister of Colleges and Universities for addressing trade-offs between quality, access and funding.

In 1987 the Council of Regents (COR) assumed a new role — one of providing the Minister with policy advice on medium-term and long-term issues affecting the college system. Vision 2000 represents a major initiative of COR in this new role. However, certain basic issues require consistent and regular analysis; solutions are not permanent — those offered today may not remain appropriate five years later. As stressed in the previous section, the college system has not had in place the necessary mechanisms for undertaking strategic planning. To ensure that this gap does not remain, we are recommending that COR establish a College System Strategic Planning Committee. We believe this will provide COR and the college system with an effective mechanism for ongoing policy research.

The experience of Vision 2000 has demonstrated that through collaborative efforts of the various stakeholders a better understanding of central issues facing the college system is achieved. Accordingly, we believe it is important that members of the Strategic Planning Committee be drawn from college faculty, college support staff, college administrators and relevant government departments, including COR. In addition, support for the Committee should be provided through staff at COR, in partnership with the staff of MCU and the colleges.

The Committee should be a working committee — one which produces substantive analyses and policy advice.

Through its research and consultation, the Committee should be in contact with the various stakeholders served by the colleges, such as students, employers, and various communities (for example, groups with special access concerns and needs). This approach would ensure that the Committee does not operate in isolation, and would allow for the perspectives and knowledge of the various constituencies to be taken into account.

As part of its initial work, the Committee might undertake to determine what it would cost per student for colleges to be institutions "that would be regarded as near the margin between inadequacy and acceptability."[57] This project, of necessity, would focus attention on the development of indicators of quality as well as require, at a macro-level, an assessment of what constitutes efficient provision of training.

The results of this exercise would serve as a *minimal* benchmark against which college revenues per student could be compared and would provide a means for monitoring and evaluating the level of support being provided to colleges. This is particularly important in light of the proposals in Chapter 4, concerning the broadening of the curriculum and the establishment of system-wide program standards.

In the beginning, the Committee should also develop a plan for systematically obtaining, from the college system and its external environment, comprehensive information, both quantitative and qualitative, for the analysis of issues related to quality, access and efficiency. Much information is

---

[57] Howard R. Bowen, *The Costs of Higher Education - How Much Do Colleges and Universities Spend per Student and How Much Should They Spend?* (San Francisco: Jossey-Bass Inc., 1980), p. 234.

already being collected, either by individual colleges or system-wide, but these data pertain primarily to full-time, post-secondary activities.

Additional data collection will need to be undertaken. Certain indices relating to program quality will become available as a result of the work of the College Standards and Accreditation Council (CSAC). But there are also serious gaps in the data necessary for the examination of access issues. Better information is required on the types and number of applicants gaining and not gaining admission to college courses and programs, population groups who appear to be underrepresented in the college system and part-time learners. While the focus of the Committee's activity must be on the analyses of a variety of data and on the dissemination of information across the system, it is also important to fill the gaps in the available data.

To ensure wide dissemination of its work, the Strategic Planning Committee, through COR, should provide an annual report to the Minister and to the college council and board of governors of each college. This report should summarize the major analytic issues examined by the Committee and the ensuing policy advice.

In the past, advocacy on behalf of the system has been severely limited by inadequate analyses of many of the fundamental issues facing the colleges. In addition to being of direct benefit to government decision-makers, we expect the analyses and advice offered by the Strategic Planning Committee will allow COR and other groups within the college system to be more effective in their advisory and advocacy roles.

Government funding: Matters of levels and stability

In the preceding chapters, we have recommended a number of major directions for the college system which, when implemented, will result in enhancing the quality of, and access to, college programs. To effectively implement these changes will require a long-term commitment on the part of both government and the college community — including a commitment to a more stable funding environment than that experienced over the past decade.

It will also be necessary to establish priorities with respect to the pace at which the system pursues each of the major directions. Enrolment demand is projected to be relatively stable until the mid-1990s, but to increase quite substantially during the remainder of decade.[58] This may provide the opportunity, in the immediate future, for greater investment in changes related to enhancing the quality of college programs. Making this investment would place the colleges in a better position to respond to the diverse and expanding enrolment demand projected for the latter half of the decade.

---

[58] David Foot and Maia MacNiven, "The Determinants of Enrolment Rates and Enrolments in Ontario Community Colleges," in *Empirical Features of the College System. Background Papers* (Toronto: Ontario Council of Regents, 1990), p. 12. The projections suggest the potential for steadily increasing demand beginning in 1994, provided that the system can accommodate the needs of non-traditional and older learners.

The next decade will be a crucial period of transition. During this time, to enhance both quality and opportunity, the college community, in partnership with government, must:

- redesign college curricula to meet identifiable standards;
- develop alternative methods for delivering programs;
- accelerate the professional development of college staff;
- develop and expand preparatory offerings;
- provide incentives for colleges to share specialized resources;
- develop further links with schools and universities; and
- evaluate progress in meeting specific targets set for these objectives.

Vision 2000 acknowledges that the variability of funding has posed a significant challenge to the colleges' ability to fulfil their educational mandate. We recognize that some fluctuations in the quantity, quality and price of educational services demanded of the colleges will always be present. Vision 2000 believes, however, that the Ontario government must make a greater effort to put college revenue on a more planned and stable footing.

 Recommendation 29

The Ministry of Colleges and Universities should review the structure of its funding to the colleges in order to provide a funding mechanism which:
- **explicitly considers both access and quality;**
- **reduces counter-productive enrolment competition among the colleges;**
- **provides greater stability in the funding provided to each college by dampening the effects of enrolment changes on a college's grant; and**
- **continues to provide predictability and promote efficiency while strengthening accountability in the use of public resources.**

Vision 2000 is not recommending a specific structure for funding. However, we offer three approaches or options for consideration and further dialogue between the system and government:

- adjusting parameters within the existing funding mechanism;
- establishing a floor for per-student funding; and
- developing a funding system based on expenditure "envelopes."

These options, which address one or more of the objectives outlined in Recommendation 29, are not intended to be exhaustive, but rather illustrative of different approaches.

Option 1: Adjusting the existing funding formula

As outlined above, the current mechanism provides for each college's grant to be allocated on the basis of its share of system activity in the period two and three years earlier. The grant share is based on historical activity for several reasons. Prior years' activity is known with certainty, so reliance on historical activity lessens the need for in-year adjustments to colleges' grants and permits reasonably accurate projections of colleges' grants two years in advance. Two additional and important reasons for using historical activity are:

- A college experiencing a decline in its share of system activity is provided some time to make the necessary adjustments to its operations. While its share of activity is in decline, its grant share will exceed its current activity share.

- A college intending to increase its share of system activity must plan its growth, as its grant share will be less than its current activity share over the period when its activity share is increasing.

The greater the number of years used in calculating the historical activity base, the greater the dampening effect on a college's current grant of changes in its share of system activity. Thus, one suggestion would be to add an additional year to the activity calculations to further reduce the immediate effects of enrolment changes on a college's revenue.

Another possibility would be to limit the range of percentage changes in grants among the colleges in any given year. In the past, when the range of percentage changes in grants was deemed to be unacceptable, the Ministry has reduced the range by reallocating funds from those colleges receiving the largest increases to those receiving the smallest increases (or declines). This type of adjustment has been ad hoc, in that there are no formal rules governing what specific circumstances dictate its application. Formally incorporating this adjustment into the mechanism might be beneficial.

Either suggestion might help to address Recommendation 29's goals of providing greater stability and predictability in grants and of reducing counter-productive enrolment competition. These changes would not explicitly address quality, but it is reasonable to expect some benefits from them. Neither of these suggested changes, however, would alter the basic principle underlying the current mechanism; namely, that grants should reflect each college's share of activity.

Option 2: Establishing a floor for per-student funding

In an effort to focus on quality, it may be necessary for the government to establish a floor below which its real funding per student at each college should not fall.[59] The 1986 faculty workload provisions limit the student-teacher ratio to some extent and therefore determine a large portion of per-student expenditures. However, in and of itself, this is not sufficient to ensure that the funding per student is adequate to ensure quality. Other factors affecting quality, such as the adequacy of instructional equipment, mode of delivery and program hours, and faculty development, remain subject to variations in the level of funding. In establishing a floor, consideration could be given to the broad range of factors affecting quality, whether contractually determined or otherwise.

The Strategic Planning Committee, proposed in Recommendation 28, could be responsible for undertaking the analysis necessary to determine the minimum acceptable level of per-student

---

[59] In a more technical sense, we should be referring to an acceptable level of expenditure per student, which would take into account that expenditures are supported not only by government operating grants but also by other sources such as tuition fees and college reserves. Also, given differences among colleges in the scale and geographic location of their operations, the floor for per-student expenditures (funding) would not be the same at each college.

funding, and recommending revisions as circumstances change. Among these circumstances would be the potential effects on program costs of curriculum changes, the introduction of alternative delivery modes, and changes in the literacy levels of students entering college.

To ensure that a college's funding per student did not fall below this specified value, one of two major changes to the existing method of funding appears to be necessary. At one extreme, total funding could be open-ended — the government would agree to, at minimum, fund whatever enrolment a college achieved at the college's specified per-student rate. At another extreme, if the current practice of distributing the system's (pre-determined) operating grant through the funding mechanism were continued, annual enrolment maxima could be established for each college, such that no college reaching its enrolment ceiling would fall below the agreed-upon floor for per-student funding. Both approaches present dilemmas which would need to be addressed in the process of determining and implementing a floor.

Adopting the principle that funding per student should not fall below a specified level would focus greater attention on quality. This focus on quality might also help to preserve college enrolment rates; in the long run, a failure to maintain quality will lead both the government and students to become increasingly disenchanted with the college system.

Option 3: Envelope or targeted funding

With the scope of changes we envision for the college system and the ever-present limits on the availability of resources, it may be appropriate for the government to introduce an envelope system of funding. Under such a system, separate funding envelopes are established, with each envelope being dedicated to a specific purpose or function.

This approach would facilitate government leadership and the pursuit of the renewed mandate recommended in this report. For the college system, the pace of change along any particular direction would depend, in part at least, on the funds allocated by the government to the associated envelope. An envelope structure of funding would also provide a means by which the government could better ensure that each college was moving at an appropriate pace with respect to each priority area.

The envelope structure of funding has been the basis of university funding in Ontario in recent years. In 1987/88, the year in which envelopes began to be used in a significant way, funding for the universities flowed from five envelopes:

- a basic grants envelope;
- an enrolment adjustment/accessibility envelope;
- a mission related, institution-specific envelope (e.g. funding for bilingualism and serving Northern communities);
- a research overhead/infrastructure envelope; and
- a program adjustment envelope (e.g. funding to assist with program closures and start-ups, and with programs jointly offered by universities).

Use of an envelope system of funding would not be entirely foreign to the college system. The vast majority of college operating funds have been provided in the form of general-purpose operating grants, which supply funds in support of college operating expenditures to be used at the discretion of the colleges. However, about 5 per cent of college operating revenues have been provided in the form of specific-purpose grants, such as targeted funds to support the provision of services to special needs students and funds for the purchase of instructional equipment.

Expanding the use of funding envelopes might be perceived to reduce somewhat the autonomy and flexibility colleges have to make their own allocations of funds. However, as an interim measure, structuring funding in this manner does have substantial appeal, given the nature of the changes that the college system will be undertaking in the 1990s. If this approach to funding were adopted, funding might fall into the following five envelope categories.

Basic operating grants envelope: This envelope would be used to fund the basic costs — faculty, administrative and support staff, heat and light, for example — associated with the instructional services provided by colleges. If the university model were followed, the amount received by each college from this envelope would remain relatively constant, in real terms, from one year to another, provided that a college's weighted enrolment remained within a corridor (i.e. plus or minus x per cent of a predetermined base level of enrolment, for example, average enrolment over the past three years). Or one might achieve a similar degree of stability by distributing this funding through the existing distribution mechanism, altered to incorporate one of the alternatives suggested in Option 1.

Funding for most of the remaining four envelopes would come from two sources: a portion of the existing general purpose operating grant would be assigned to these envelopes; and new operating funds provided to the college system by the government could be allocated to these envelopes.

Accessibility envelope: This envelope would be used to fund enrolment growth beyond some enrolment corridor (or base enrolment) established for each college. Funding from this envelope could be distributed on the basis of each eligible college's share of enrolment growth. If a college experienced a decline in enrolment which caused it to fall outside its enrolment corridor, its basic operating grant would be adjusted downward, and the accessibility envelope or other envelopes could be augmented by this amount.

Credential program development envelope: This envelope would be used to fund both provincial and local activities related to the proposed restructuring of college credential programs. At the provincial level, funds could be allocated to CSAC to establish system-wide program standards and to undertake program reviews. In funding the development of program standards, allocations could be spread over several years; initially they might be directed at pilot projects in a limited number of program areas. In addition, where initiatives involving the development of new forms of program delivery or professional development of college staff are undertaken collectively by the system, funds from this envelope could be used to support these activities.

At the local college level, funds could be directed at extraordinary expenditures related to curriculum revisions and professional development of staff necessitated by new program standards;

the introduction of alternative modes of program delivery; and costs associated with closing programs and starting up new credential programs.

Preparatory programs and student services envelope: This envelope would be dedicated to supporting the development of college preparatory offerings (the ongoing instructional costs associated with these courses would be funded through the basic grants envelope); the development and expansion of student assessment and placement services; and the provision of services to special needs students (e.g. support services for students with a physical disability).

Linkage envelope: This envelope would be used to fund the initial costs of projects which involve the sharing of specialized resources among colleges, such as the development of a program to be jointly offered by two or more colleges. Also eligible for funding would be projects developing links between colleges and schools, such as co-operative efforts by local school boards and a college to develop curricula in the secondary schools and colleges which improve the transition from secondary school to college. Projects developing links between colleges and universities, such as the development of custom degree-completion programs for college graduates attending university (like Lakehead University's engineering program), could also be funded.

In addition to these envelopes, the existing targeted funding for instructional equipment and capital expenditures would need to be continued.

In distributing funds from the envelopes, a variety of approaches might be used. In some instances, distribution on the basis of each college's share of system enrolment would be appropriate. In other cases, however, it may be beneficial to distribute the funds on the basis of a competitive bidding process or a matching formula. For example, if a college allocated funds from its basic operating grant for the professional development of staff, additional funds might be provided from the program development envelope to augment these professional development activities. (Specific initiatives with respect to human resource development are discussed in the next chapter. Although these initiatives were not necessarily designed with an envelope structure of funding in mind, this form of funding would be appropriate for at least some of the proposed initiatives.)

If an expanded envelope structure of funding were adopted, COR should undertake to provide advice to the Minister on the amount of funds to allocate to each envelope, and the methods for distributing funds from each envelope. COR, with input from both CSAC and the Strategic Planning Committee, would be in a position to integrate the analyses and viewpoints of the various stakeholders and to provide an assessment of whether outcome targets established under the envelope structure were being met.

Co-ordination of funding

Whatever the approach to funding provided by MCU, the programs currently funded by MSD, other provincial ministries and CEIC must also be considered. MCU has historically played the central role of providing governmental guidance and support to the college system. The primary relationship between the colleges and MCU remains, but increasingly the colleges are responding to training initiatives supported by a number of other ministries, both at the provincial and federal levels.

Because of the cyclical demand for skills training, many of the short programs sponsored by these other provincial ministries and the federal government are subject to unstable funding. No long-term commitment to funding exists, and training programs to meet identified government priorities are often launched on very short notice, then cancelled or significantly reduced in scope with equally short notice. Recent examples include changes to Futures and Ontario Basic Skills, programs funded by MSD. These conditions contribute to similar problems concerning the relationship among quality, access and funding as those described in relation to MCU-funded post-secondary programs. Many of these non-MCU activities have been ineffectively co-ordinated with MCU. This has limited MCU's ability to provide the college system with an environment that is sufficiently stable and conducive to the provision of high-quality training.

In addition, as discussed in Chapter 5, the decision by the federal government to increase its support of skills training in the private sector has also affected the colleges. This policy change has led to reductions in federal funds flowing to the colleges and uncertainty about the levels of federal funding which will be available to the colleges in the future. Under these conditions it is difficult for the colleges to develop a clear and coherent mission – programs are continually at risk and staff morale and commitment suffers. The problems are further complicated by the fact that the provincial ministry (MSD) which is responsible for negotiations with the federal government is not the same ministry charged with ensuring the well-being of the colleges (MCU).

If the colleges are to be effective instruments of public policy, they should not have to rely on uncoordinated funding sources, each of which may have different expectations and policy goals. We believe that greater involvement of the colleges and MCU in the development of provincial policies and funding arrangements affecting skills training, as well as in federal/provincial negotiations on skills training, would help to alleviate many of the existing problems.

 Recommendation 30

> **The Ontario government should introduce a more participatory and co-ordinated system for developing government policies, initiatives, and funding arrangements affecting skills training provided by the colleges.**

Tuition fees

Changing circumstances will require a reassessment of current tuition fee structures, within both the college and the university sectors. The quality-access-funding trade-offs necessitate an examination of the rationale, objectives and impact of the current levels of tuition fee subsidies.

In 1989/90, the standard tuition fee for a full-time, post-secondary student attending a college is $685 for two semesters. Annual university fees for undergraduate students range from $882 to $2,096, depending on the program and institution, with most fees around $1,500.

In the colleges, the standard tuition fee amounts to approximately $0.85 to $1.00 per hour of instruction and represents, on average, about 11 to 12 per cent of college operating revenues (standard fee plus MCU operating grant to the college) attributable to the presence of a full-time student. The standard fee applies to all full-time students (except international students), whatever their choice of program and thus whatever the program cost per student contact hour. In addition to the tuition fee, colleges, as well as the universities, may also charge students for non-tuition-related items (e.g. the costs of learning materials, equipment and clothing retained by the student).

For part-time students enrolled in provincially supported college courses the fee is $1.60 per contact hour. This fee represents about 25 per cent of college operating revenues (fee plus MCU grant) attributable to the presence of such a part-time student. In courses not eligible for provincial funding (e.g. general interest courses), part-time fees may be whatever a college deems appropriate.

International students attending a college on a full-time basis pay a standard fee of $5,705 — a fee which is intended to reflect the full per-student operating expenditures of colleges. Fees for international students attending university generally range from $5,053 to $9,326, depending on the program and institution.

The post-secondary system will need to address how changes in fee levels would affect access to post-secondary education and institutional revenues. Limitations on the ability of government to provide additional resources to the college and university sectors, and expected changes in the composition and size of the post-secondary student body, require an examination of student fees.

As previously noted, older students are likely to represent an increasing proportion of a growing student body. Some of these older students will be attending part-time, while working; others will be attending full-time and spending their savings from past employment; still others will be laid-off workers or persons on fixed incomes, attempting to improve their economic circumstances through further education. And with the aging of the population, demands on other publicly supported services, such as health services, will increase significantly in the coming years, and thus possibly constrain the government's funding of post-secondary institutions.

Another important reason for undertaking a study of tuition fees is the concern that students' decisions regarding the type of post-secondary institution to attend may not be conforming to societal needs. This study could examine the contention of some educators that a greater percentage of post-secondary students should be selecting a college education.

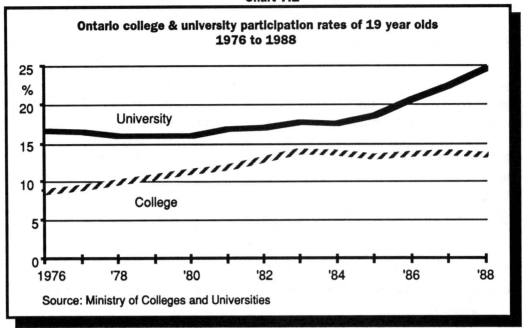

Chart 7.2

**Ontario college & university participation rates of 19 year olds
1976 to 1988**

Source: Ministry of Colleges and Universities

The study might also examine the extent to which altering the distribution of students between colleges and universities could be achieved through changing the existing relationship between college and university fees.[60]

 Recommendation 31

The government should initiate a study, encompassing both the college and university sectors, to assess the impact of alternative tuition fee and student assistance policies on access and institutional revenues.

The proposed assessment of tuition fees should examine both full-time and part-time fees and take into account a number of factors, including:

- the economic and social objectives underlying the level of subsidy inherent in the college and university fee structures;

- the effectiveness of current fee and student assistance policies in meeting these objectives;[61]

---

[60] In a research paper prepared for Vision 2000, Noemi Stokes and David Foot analyze factors (e.g. family background, student characteristics, institutional characteristics, and financial factors) that affect the type of post-secondary institution (college versus university) a student selects. Based on 1984 student data collected by Statistics Canada, they estimate that, for example, a 7 per cent increase in university fees, holding college fees constant, would lower the percentage of post-secondary students selecting university over college by 1 per cent (or 0.6 percentage points), from 62.5 per cent (the 1984 percentage) to 61.9 per cent. See: N. Stokes and D. Foot, *Regional Differences in the Determinants of Post-Secondary Educational Choice in Canada: Community College versus University* (unpublished paper submitted to Vision 2000, Toronto, 1989).

[61] In addition, consideration might also be given to expanding the assessment of student assistance practices to include an examination of policies governing students enrolled in private vocational schools.

- the impact of changing demographics on the future composition of the post-secondary student body and their ability to pay for their education; and

- the impact of alternative fee levels and structures and various student assistance schemes (grant and loan) on:

    a) overall access to post-secondary institutions;

    b) the social and private rates of return from a college and university education and the distribution of students between the college and university sectors; and

    c) the total investment (public and individual) in post-secondary education.

The alternatives considered should include:

- maintaining, increasing, reducing or eliminating fees in a manner which either maintains or alters the existing relationship between college and university fees;

- differentiating fees by level of study (i.e. one fee for first year, another for second year, and so on);

- establishing different fees for different programs, with fee differentials being related to differences in programs' instructional costs and/or differences among programs in the rates of return to graduates; and

- introducing an income-based contingent repayment loan scheme.

It is important to note that the university sector has already begun an assessment of tuition fee policies.[62] It would be unfortunate if college tuition policies were altered as result of a review which focussed exclusively on university fees. The colleges' role in post-secondary education is quite different from that of the universities, as is the make-up of the student body (e.g. in terms of family income). Therefore, in recognition of this and the potential impact of college-university fee differentials on post-secondary students' choice of institution, we have proposed a study which examines college and university fees simultaneously.

7.5 Sharing Specialized Resources

An important characteristic of a college *system* is the sharing of specialized resources. Many colleges have already developed their own areas of expertise as part of their response to their community, be it local or provincial, such as the woodwork centre at Conestoga and the comprehensive program in natural resources at Sir Sandford Fleming.[63]

---

[62] David A. A. Stager, *Focus on Fees — Alternative Policies for University Tuition Fees* (Toronto: Council of Ontario Universities, 1989).

[63] For a discussion of some areas of program concentration see the section called Regional Distribution of Enrolment by Program and Breadth of Programming by Region in "The College System — An Empirical Snapshot," in *Empirical Features of the College System. Background Papers* (Toronto: Ontario Council of Regents, 1990), pp. 22-24.

In the previous sections we have underscored the need for co-operation in the context of the trade-offs inherent in the quality-access-funding relationship. We also noted that Ontario's need for college education is growing and that safeguarding and improving quality is imperative. Given these needs, Vision 2000 believes that in order to realize greater access and higher quality within fiscal limits, colleges will have to make sharing specialized resources more of a priority. Only by being aware of what other colleges are providing and by engaging in co-operative activities can each college, and the system as a whole, develop effective strategic plans for coping with finite resources.

Being responsive to local needs will, we are convinced, continue to be one of the greatest assets of colleges as public educational institutions. However, developing local expertise also implies that not all programs are available in every part of the province. As more colleges develop areas of specialization — for example, a particular field relevant to disadvantaged learners or emerging areas of the service or manufacturing sectors — the challenge is to make these special programs accessible to students across Ontario.

There is also the prospect that as local needs change, so too will the range of educational services offered by specific colleges. The impact of these changes on access must be minimized. Thus, even though decisions about which programs to curtail or suspend must be shaped at the local level, the decisions should take into account shared information and system-wide possibilities which minimize their impact on local access. Our goal must be to ensure students every opportunity to find and pursue their educational aspirations.

Some of the steps needed to realize a system where specialized resources are effectively shared have already been taken. Numerous colleges are currently engaged in projects which involve shared or joint use of resources. However, there is no open and organized forum in place to help all colleges plan and co-ordinate the sharing of specialized resources.

 Recommendation 32

> **The Council of Regents, through its Strategic Planning Committee, should develop and recommend a mechanism to co-ordinate information and plans relevant to the sharing of specialized resources among the colleges.**

COR must seek to establish methods for sharing resources which safeguard the needs of local communities. The work of the CSAC program councils proposed in Chapter 4 should provide valuable information which could assist COR in its role of facilitating an appropriate sharing of resources.

Vision 2000 foresees COR encouraging colleges to share specialized resources in a number of different ways. For instance:

- One college may establish itself as an expert in serving a specific learning-disadvantaged group. This college might develop training material and sell it to other colleges in the province.

- The experts from a specialized program at one college could engage in job exchanges with individuals from other colleges.

- A number of colleges might develop a unique computer-based learning program for a particular course, which is then shared across the system.

- Two or more colleges might engage in joint program development which then allows students enrolled at one institution to attend another institution for part of their studies (e.g. the first two years in College X; the third year in College Y).

- A few colleges might jointly develop a specific educational service, such as an international trade tour for employers, which could then be marketed by the system as a whole.

Vision 2000 predicts that as the colleges continue to work together as a system, other new ways of sharing specialized resources will come to light.

Most importantly, we believe that sharing resources is an effective way for the entire system to use limited funding to maintain quality and accessibility. Addressing the trade-offs inherent in the relationships among these variables is not an easy task. Given the quality, access and funding challenges we have identified, Ontario's colleges must pool their energies and expertise.

8

Investing in College Educators, Curriculum and Delivery

8.1 Preamble

Continuous retraining is now generally recognized as necessary for all workplaces. Colleges are no exception. Teachers, staff and administrators must themselves be continuously learning. Those who create the learning environment must be involved in renewing their ability to serve changing student needs. If our goal is for students to be innovative lifelong learners, then the instructors and the college as a whole should lead by example. For Ontario's colleges — whose mission is to educate — the lessons must begin at home.

Vision 2000's consultations underscored the importance of the teaching and learning environment. It is of paramount importance to every major constituency, including faculty, staff, students, employers, labour and community groups. Realizing a positive teaching and learning experience depends, in large measure, upon a commitment to the continued development of the knowledge and skills of all those who work in our colleges.

Renewal must be embedded in the organization's culture. Particularly in these times of financial restraint, it is crucial that college presidents and boards of governors lead the way through their own behaviour and personal commitment to professional development.

Currently, many colleges engage in extensive professional development activities. These programs have been beneficial for participants. However, even in the more committed institutions, human resource development (HRD) programs are often intermittent and not sufficiently integrated into the functioning of the institution. Unfortunately, some colleges, like many other employers, still retain a perspective which views professional development as a cost rather than an investment.

The need for human resource development is an ongoing one, and the need is augmented when there are significant changes in the existing workforce. This will occur in the colleges in the next 10 to 15 years because of large numbers of retirements. By the year 2000, over one-fifth of the current teachers and administrators in the system will be 65 or older; and by 2005, about half of the current

and administrators will have retired. As the year 2000 approaches, the largest number of
in terms of five-year age groups, will be in the 50-54 age range.

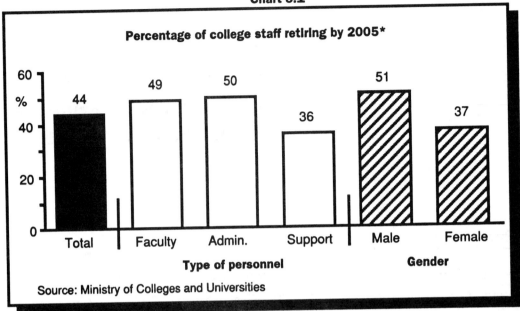

Chart 8.1

Percentage of college staff retiring by 2005*

Source: Ministry of Colleges and Universities

*These estimates assume that the average age of retirement is 62. The estimates relate to the 15,764 full-time employees of the college system who are enrolled in the College Pension Plan. Excluded are approximately 400 faculty and 100 administrators who are members of the Teachers' Superannuation Fund; these excluded employees would tend, on average, to be older than those belonging to the College Pension Plan.

The retirement of significant numbers of college employees will have consequences for professional development and renewal in the system. There will be more pressure to keep older teachers current in their fields; to ensure that the colleges' workforce reflects the demographic and cultural diversity of the community; and to provide adequate training for new teachers, administrators and support staff hired to replace retirees.

Provincially, the importance of human resource development as an investment has been reinforced by both the colleges' Council of Presidents (COP) and the Premier's Council. Indeed, COP recently initiated a project to facilitate staff development on a system-wide basis. The goals of this project, entitled "Human Resources in the Third Decade," are to evaluate current HRD activities; to co-ordinate and initiate local, regional and provincial HRD activities; and to develop and provide program information, ideas and training materials on HRD.

The progress report *A Blueprint for Human Resource Development in the Third Decade* (March 1989) states:

> The strengths that will enable the colleges to face the challenges of the future will lie ... in their human resources ... Today's colleges are complex ... striving to adapt to increasingly diverse societal demands in ways that are frequently blurred and reactive ... Colleges have been required to adjust to the needs of greater proportions of non-traditional learners. Upgrading and retraining programs, employment equity programs for women, immigrant and minority groups, seniors, those with environmental and other challenges, have all demanded new and flexible responses

from the colleges ... If colleges are to provide relevant training to graduates and custom training for businesses to compete in the economic market, they must demonstrate, in-house, the kinds of programs that they promote to their communities ... There is an overwhelming need for system-wide planning, co-ordination, and co-operation for the development of the colleges' most important resource — its people — for the years ahead. (p.1)

For Vision 2000, the "HRD in the Third Decade" project represents an excellent start toward increasing the colleges' commitment to HRD. This project has already generated impressive system-wide and regional activities in the areas of leadership training, HRD training, teaching excellence, and career development. Further development of this initiative will be contingent on greater stakeholder involvement (including full union participation); more direct financial support by the government and the colleges; and an increased recognition of the emerging skill needs identified by Vision 2000. This chapter offers a number of recommendations which aim to enhance the developmental opportunities of all college personnel.

8.2 Challenges for Human Resource Development

As the colleges strive to become model centres of lifelong learning for both students and staff, HRD activities — in whatever form — will have to focus on helping colleges deal with the implications of the following challenges.

- To develop and adapt to new program standards and criteria for quality assurance.

- To ensure that the content of college programs is current and relevant.

- To achieve a proper balance between narrowly defined career education and training, and generic skills and general education.

- To improve the curriculum and program links between schools, colleges and universities.

- To increase the colleges' ability to provide advanced training.

- To develop a more flexible, learner-centred approach to learning.

- To ensure that faculty possess the requisite knowledge and skills to serve the specific needs of of a diverse population of part-time adult learners.

- To ensure more effective use of new technologies for the full range of educational services — from distance learning to assessment.

- To increase the colleges' capacity to engage in community partnerships and offer consultant services which assist with the diffusion and transfer of technology and expertise.

- To support and expand international activity in the colleges.

- To increase colleges' ability to engage in partnership activity with the local, provincial and global community.

- To ensure sensitivity to issues related to equity and the environment.

- To ensure that there is appropriate planning for the large number of faculty retirements expected in the next 10 to 15 years.

Challenges of this range and magnitude are both daunting and exciting. The excitement arises as we envisage the potential for colleges to play a pivotal role in responding to these challenges. The trepidation stems from the extent of the changes required at a time when resources are scarce and time horizons are short. For Vision 2000 it is critically important that in responding to these challenges the colleges and the government target policies and programs to ensure the most effective use of human and financial resources. A co-ordinated and precisely defined approach toward human resource development, in its broadest sense, is a precondition for realizing the much-needed social and economic benefits of investing in Ontario's colleges.

8.3 A Framework for Investment In HRD

Turning the challenges posed by the preceding list into practical policy will be a major test for the colleges during the course of the next ten years. In this section we propose a framework for orienting the necessary investments in HRD and related activity.

In order to realize the renewed mandate, colleges working together and with the support of the provincial government will be required to make major investments in:

- faculty, support and administrative staff — through **human resource development** initiatives;

- programs and courses which are current, relevant and of a high standard of quality — through **curriculum development** initiatives; and

- modes of instruction which provide the flexibility to meet the needs of learners and employers — through **alternative delivery** initiatives.

These areas of investment reinforce one another. Curriculum development and alternative delivery are an integral part of cultivating a wide and productive range of human resource development opportunities. These activities will, in part, be a natural outcome of the need for faculty to exchange information, collaborate and generally find new ways to develop and present curriculum.

Take the case of a graphic arts teacher working with a computer technology instructor to design computer-based desktop publishing tutorials (combining curriculum development with human resource development). This courseware could then be used on the student's home computer or at the college's facility when it is convenient for the student (alternative delivery).

Other instructors, perhaps from three distinct fields such as technology, English and computer science, might become involved in a consultative project for a local business. They could help with design and problem-solving, thereby transferring their expertise in designing computer courseware to update an employee's knowledge in the workplace (alternative delivery). Working with a business will help increase the college's links to the community. It will also enable teachers to better understand the problems encountered by business, improving the faculty's knowledge of the discipline (human resource development). The instructors can later translate the results of their experience into new material for their students (curriculum development).

Vision 2000 recognizes that colleges are already involved in this type of activity. What we are advocating is increasing the commitment to initiatives in these areas in ways which respond to the challenges of the renewed mandate. Increased staff development, curriculum development and alternative delivery will require commitments and initiatives at the local and provincial levels. Only partnerships — between colleges and the government, colleges and their staff, colleges and the community, colleges and other colleges — will make these investments sustainable and successful.

In the next section, we discuss the responsibility for human resource development at the local level. Then we turn to provincial initiatives aimed at supporting HRD in the colleges and providing a system-wide infrastructure to generate widespread innovations in curriculum development and alternative delivery. Finally, the last two sections of this chapter address two important ways of improving organizational effectiveness in the colleges: applied scholarship and performance evaluation.

8.4 Increasing Commitment at the Local Level

We see a primary role for the colleges in developing their own human resources. In the past, colleges have varied in their funding commitments to HRD. Funds for human resource development are usually allocated from colleges' general operating revenues, which has meant that HRD is often one of the first budgets to be cut back in times of financial restraint. Over a prolonged period, neglect of human resource development can have consequences for the quality of the education provided, as well as employee morale.

Regardless of what has happened in the past, it is now essential that all colleges demonstrate an increased commitment by setting clear and specific targets for expenditures on human resource development. Boards of governors must show leadership by providing a clear focus, stable funding, and a consistent commitment to HRD. They must also develop plans for HRD through a collaborative process involving all relevant stakeholders.

Vision 2000 believes that human resource development is fundamental to other aspects of organizational development and effectiveness. Development of curriculum and alternative delivery methods will be based on the expertise, creativity and commitment of the people who "deliver" the knowledge to learners.

We are encouraged by the fact that a few of the colleges have set targets for HRD expenditures and have designated between one percent and two per cent of their total budgets for this purpose. We believe this is a worthwhile goal, particularly when HRD should include the entire college organization.

Recommendation 33

Every college's board of governors should reinforce Vision 2000's major objectives through its human resources planning by undertaking initiatives such as:

- setting clear budgetary targets for increasing the share of funds devoted to human resource development (HRD);

- including a section on HRD in the annual report to the Minister, which summarizes the college's progress in developing and implementing HRD policies and practices designed to achieve the objectives of the renewed mandate; and

- developing policy guidelines (to complement existing professional development leave policies) which provide regular opportunities and direct encouragement for external work experience, job exchanges or international activity for faculty, support staff and administrators.

Vision 2000 believes that colleges must strive for a two per cent target for HRD spending on the basis of two factors: the existing precedent set by several colleges, and the relatively small proportion of the total college budget available for discretionary non-salaried expenditures. Movement toward a two per cent target is essential if the colleges are to realize the necessary changes in human resource development and associated curriculum and delivery reform. It will also be essential for provincial resources, including explicit government funding, to match the commitment made by local colleges. We recommend in the next section that the colleges be supported by additional provincial resources and system-wide co-ordination of HRD efforts.

Having called upon the colleges to set budgetary objectives for HRD, it is also important that the college system be able to improve its commitment through shared information. We have therefore recommended that each college's annual report to the Minister include a section on HRD. The goal is to provide ways of gaining recognition and pooling resources.

We also believe that one of the most effective means of renewal is for educators to participate in external work experience, job exchanges and international activity. These types of professional development provide excellent reciprocal benefits to both teachers and the recipients of their expertise in other organizations or other nations. For example, curriculum links are strengthened when a college teacher exchanges jobs with a high school teacher. When an exchange takes place with an innovative educational institution, or when a teacher works abroad (for example, under a program set up by the Association of Canadian Community Colleges), college educators provide their expertise and gain working knowledge of new delivery methods and other cultures. The ultimate benefactors are students, whose learning is infused with their teachers' fresh knowledge.

Current policies for encouraging faculty involvement in professional development outside the college are somewhat limited. As it stands now, the collective agreement and other mechanisms provide faculty with professional development days. After a certain period of service, staff are eligible for year-long leaves. These extended leaves can be taken more than once, but only if a specified amount of time has occurred between them. There is a need to complement these professional development initiatives with more frequent opportunities, perhaps of two or three months' duration, which allow for participants to become immersed in another environment.

8.5 Increasing Commitment at the Provincial Level

Efforts by individual colleges to develop an institutional culture of HRD must be complemented by commitments at the provincial level. This section offers some proposals for fostering HRD, curriculum development and alternative delivery with the support and sharing of resources that are available at the provincial level.

The Council of Presidents' "HRD in the Third Decade" project marks a new beginning for professional development activities at a provincial, system-wide level. Vision 2000 supports the project's work and believes the process would be significantly enhanced if the Steering Committee included broader stakeholder participation, specifically, greater participation of faculty and support staff.

The "HRD in the Third Decade" project has addressed the need to balance and co-ordinate provincial activity with appropriate regional and local activity. Vision 2000 believes this process merits further support and expansion in the context of the challenges posed by the renewed college mandate.

Recommendation 34

The Ontario Government should work with all college stakeholders to establish and fund:
- **a permanent Professional Development Fund to reinforce and expand upon the professional development efforts of the HRD in the Third Decade project; and**
- **an Instructional Development Task Force to provide leadership in helping the colleges develop learner-centred curriculum and alternative delivery.**

Generally, the intent of this recommendation is to direct new funds, potentially on a matching grant or seed funding basis, for provincially approved efforts at HRD, curriculum development and alternative delivery. We believe that the criteria for allocating these funds should reflect the priorities necessary for realizing the colleges' renewed mandate. The goal is to support projects which have system-wide implications and reinforce the investments in HRD activity by the system and local boards.

The Professional Development Fund: Involving the "HRD in the Third Decade" Steering Committee in the allocation of this fund is one effective way to ensure that the sponsored projects serve provincial objectives consistent with the aims of the renewed mandate. Using this approach, the annual allocation of funds for these projects would be contingent upon the submission of a plan by the HRD Steering Committee to the Deputy Minister of the Ministry of Colleges and Universities (MCU). The implementation of these proposed funds would provide the government with an opportunity to show leadership in the development of co-ordinated HRD efforts.

Instructional Development Task Force: Specific funding schemes must also be established to help meet the urgent need for new curriculum development and delivery to meet the demands of the renewed mandate for generic skills, general education and student-centred instructional methods.

The HRD Steering Committee would be responsible for appointing a representative group of stakeholders to sit on the Task Force and for guiding the overall process. Among the aims of the Instructional Development Task Force would be to:

- work with all colleges to develop a comprehensive plan for a flexible and learner-centred system of instructional delivery, which should be implemented by 1998;

- fund college-based pilot projects on curriculum development and alternative delivery;

- develop system-wide exchange agreements to share ideas, resources and results (e.g. course modules and software);

- facilitate and establish means for innovative uses of technology for student-driven learning and distance education;

- provide seed funding for projects which enhance a college's ability to develop and sustain initiatives which will be ongoing;

- establish an Educational Courseware Institute as a joint venture between the colleges, the software/courseware industry and appropriate government ministries; and

- develop and implement curriculum design training materials and programs for college-based staff.

In previous chapters we have underscored the fact that serving lifelong learners means educational institutions must provide opportunities for students to learn in ways which suit them. Instruction should not necessarily be time-based, nor should it be solely classroom-based. New curriculum development must allow students to select from a number of individual learning activities, including segmented instructional units. In this student-oriented environment, a specified number of units would be equivalent to a course, and a specified number of courses would be equivalent to a diploma.

Changes of this magnitude in the way instruction is organized should be implemented in the very near future, but they will not happen on a sufficient scale without special attention and funding.

Provincial initiative for faculty graduate education

One important way for the Ontario government to demonstrate its commitment to HRD would be to support initiatives for the continuing formal education of college faculty. This would provide a direct way of addressing the needs of college personnel who are continuing their own formal education, or who would like to do so, in order to complement more local and informal non-credential professional development activity.

Many faculty are currently enrolled in Ontario universities as part of HRD activities, but many more are registered in American programs. This is due to the perception that U.S. institutions are more flexible with respect to delivery and providing credit for prior learning and experience.

In view of the increased emphasis on general education, generic skills and alternative delivery proposed by Vision 2000, it will be very important for faculty to have access to university-level professional development opportunities. It is also crucial to plan for the renewal of faculty that will be necessary because of retirements. Consequently, we believe it is time for the government to encourage Ontario universities to be more active in meeting the demands of college personnel for graduate level programs.

Recommendation 35

The Minister of Colleges and Universities should provide sufficient funding to enable an Ontario university (or several, working in a consortium) to develop graduate-level programs for community college personnel.

This community college educators program should be flexible and offer credit for experience. The specifications for the program should reflect the needs of the colleges and should therefore be set by the "HRD in the Third Decade" Steering Committee of COP, in conjunction with the university system. A range of joint college/university initiatives in the HRD area will be critically important for the future of Ontario's post-secondary system.

8.6 Colleges and Applied Scholarship

For many college faculty, lifelong learning involves more than attending courses and obtaining additional credentials or keeping up with the latest literature in the field. In fact, for many teachers the most effective way to stay current is to apply their knowledge through various forms of applied scholarship, or the transfer of technology and other expertise.

Vision 2000 defines applied scholarship broadly to include a range of activities, from problem-solving and the transfer or diffusion of information and technology to the development of new services and products. This definition comprises more than just the scholarship of discovering knowledge through research. It includes the scholarship of integrating knowledge (through curriculum development), applying knowledge (through service) and presenting knowledge (through teaching).[64]

A significant amount of this type of activity is already taking place in the college system. A survey conducted in 1988 reveals that in that year seven per cent of college faculty had served on the editorial board of a journal; 10 per cent had received a research grant; 17 per cent had reviewed proposals on behalf of a funding agency; 19 per cent had published an article in an academic or

---

[64] Commission on the Future of Community Colleges, *Building Communities, A Vision for a New Century* (Washington, D.C.: American Association of Community and Junior Colleges, 1988), p. 26.

professional journal; 24 per cent had published or edited, alone or in collaboration, a book or a monograph; and 30 per cent had delivered a paper at a professional meeting or conference.[65]

Many, both inside and outside the college system, firmly believe that active participation in applied scholarship and research results in better instruction. Survey data suggest that college faculty consider teaching their foremost task and want to continue to dedicate their efforts and time to instruction. But these same survey results also portray a widespread desire for a climate more hospitable toward applied scholarship.

Vision 2000 believes that faculty participation in applied scholarship and research will serve to upgrade and expand the knowledge of instructors, making their courses more current, effective and innovative. There is also evidence that encouraging involvement with discovery and innovation can lead to increased morale and job satisfaction, particularly given the manifest trend toward higher academic qualifications among college faculty.

Embedding a training culture within the college walls is essential for educational excellence. However, the benefits of applied scholarship go beyond the college and into the community. Colleges are able to and, as public institutions, obligated to contribute their expertise in meeting the research and development needs of the community.

Local communities are already reaping the benefits of utilizing the college's expertise. Business, industry, non-profit organizations and the public sector have expressed the need to establish collaborative projects with colleges. Such partnerships offer mutually beneficial learning relationships; an increase in the relevance of college services in the local community; and an increase in fee-for-service training provided on a cost-recovery basis. Vision 2000 shares the view of the Premier's Council that these activities are vitally important to Ontario's social and economic well-being.

Vision 2000 also shares the keen interest of policy-makers in the international challenges facing Ontario. We believe colleges have a contribution to make. Many colleges are already exporting some of their educational services and applied research knowledge.

For the host country, international partnerships transfer valuable knowledge and skills. The impact in Ontario is equally important and relevant. Gearing up for a more global economy and society means that the colleges need to participate in the international arena. Reaching beyond our borders allows educators to bring international perspectives to the classroom and the local community. And for students, business and the local community, developing an understanding and a strategy for competing, negotiating and working with foreign enterprises and governments is essential.

---

65 For a more detailed description of this survey, see Sandford Borins and Shirley Holloway, "Meeting the Competitive Challenge: Enhancing Applied Research in Ontario's Colleges," in *Colleges and the Changing Economy. Background Papers* (Toronto: Ontario Council of Regents, 1989), pp. 10-15.

To summarize, Vision 2000 sees applied scholarship as an important aspect of serving the colleges' constituencies — students, faculty and the community at large. We believe that efforts to encourage applied activities will not only safeguard but enhance the primacy of the colleges' teaching function.

 Recommendation 36

The colleges should work together to introduce effective means for fostering applied scholarship as a way of enhancing the primacy of the colleges' teaching function.

To facilitate this process, COP, under the leadership of its "HRD in the Third Decade" project, might convene a working group to assess various approaches to increasing faculty involvement in applied scholarship activities that contribute to the overall goal of teaching excellence. The working group should be composed of a variety of college stakeholders, including representatives of college administrators, faculty and staff, the MCU, the Ministry of Industry, Trade and Technology, employers (both public and private) and labour.

In our view, the working group's most important task would be to design policies and activities that enhance teaching capabilities by supporting local college applied scholarship. Priorities and incentives must be set in a manner which fosters a more effective learning environment for students. In this sense, the involvement of any faculty in the application and transfer of knowledge must, first and foremost, serve to enrich instruction and encourage innovative teaching.

To this end, the working group should set out a practical definition of applied scholarship; assess the specific needs for applied activity; find ways to encourage this activity; and develop an applied scholarship agenda for the entire college system. They will also be required to address the issues of faculty workload; apprehension that greater efforts at applied work will be at the expense of teaching; worries about costs to the college system and the limited funds available at a provincial level for this type of activity; concern about the division of labour between colleges and universities; and the difficulty of achieving local and system-wide co-ordination.

8.7 A Note on Performance, Development and Accountability

While each college's culture should continue to be as varied as the local communities served, our colleges should reflect common objectives and a shared sense of accountability when it comes to the professional activities of all those that work there. There should be a demonstrable, measurable and ongoing commitment to professional growth on the part of *all* who work in the colleges.

Currently the colleges vary markedly with respect to methods of evaluation for teachers, support staff and administrators. In some colleges, teachers regularly take part in formative evaluation systems which include peer input and feedback from students. Other colleges are not engaged in such activity except for the compulsory evaluation which is part of a new teacher's probationary period. All administrators, including college presidents, are supposed to receive detailed annual appraisals. But many do not. As a result, these college administrators are not afforded a detailed, constructive and effective appraisal on a regular basis. Appraisals for support staff are also irregular in the college system.

As several researchers have indicated, and common experience in many different institutions has reinforced, ineffective implementation has caused words like "evaluation" and "appraisal" to be seen in a negative light. This negative connotation pertains to most organizations, not just colleges.

Constructive evaluation methods are too often either misused or ignored. Evaluation schemes tend to be one-way and top-down. The evaluation is often carried out by individuals who have not had proper training in constructive evaluation techniques or in the coaching skills required to bring about improvements in individuals' performances. And often a new scheme of evaluation is imported into an organization for a specific target group without first introducing the critical organizational characteristics, such as support and reward systems, needed to accommodate the innovation in evaluation. Grafting even the best evaluation methodology onto a hostile, or at best neutral, environment does not work. The literature dealing with instructional evaluation provides ample evidence of such failures.[66]

Successful integration of an evaluation scheme into an organization requires that all workers are provided with opportunities to improve their performance. Rewards and support are part of the scheme. Using this type of approach, people can obtain honest and effective feedback which has no implications beyond providing directions for growth.

And as noted by Jaccaci in a recent edition of *Training and Development Journal*:

> A learning culture is one where collaborative creativity in all contexts, relationships, and experiences is a basic purpose of the culture. It is a culture where the measure of success is the combined wisdom of groups and the synergy, leadership and service of the organization as a whole. Up to now, individuals have done the learning, but in a learning culture with multiple interactions among learning groups, the whole culture learns in a self-aware, self-reflective, and creative way.[67]

The pressure in the college system to introduce student evaluations of teachers has excellent potential for reinforcing new ways of looking at evaluation and development. This type of evaluation can create a reciprocal relationship between someone providing leadership in a formal sense — the teacher — who is assisted in her/his development by those on the receiving end of that leadership — the student. However, the only way in which the developmental reciprocity between teacher and student can flourish is if the same relationship exists between the teachers and those who, in turn, lead them. For example, those administrators who wish to implement student evaluations of teachers, along with other methods, must begin by asking teachers to evaluate their administrators.

---

[66] See for instance Christopher K. Knapper, et.al., *If Teaching is Important: The evaluation of instruction in higher education* (Clarke, Irwin & Company Ltd., 1977).

[67] August T. Jaccaci, "The Social Architecture of a Learning Culture," *Training and Development Journal*, Vol. 43, No. 11 (November, 1989), p. 49-51.

Vision 2000 maintains that developing cultures which are both performance-driven and constructive will only happen if the process is first championed by college leaders. One of the best ways to accomplish this may be to have presidents initiate a process for their own performance review which involves evaluations from faculty, support staff and administrators. This would signal "everyone here is a lifelong learner, including the President."

 Recommendation 37

Each college should experiment in developing reciprocal methods of performance review which are formative in nature for all employees. The process for developing these procedures should itself be collaborative in nature.

9

Role of College Boards and the Ontario Council of Regents

9.1 Preamble

Throughout this report we have affirmed that college leaders will be key players in moving the college system in the new directions described by Vision 2000. We have discussed the roles of the colleges' boards of governors and the Council of Regents (COR). In this chapter we briefly summarize the expectations Vision 2000 holds for boards of governors and COR in order to realize the new directions we have proposed for the college system.

9.2 Local Boards of Governors

Local boards of governors will have a crucial role to play in pursuing the major goals of assuring quality and enhancing opportunity in their colleges. While it is understood that numerous boards are making excellent progress in preparing for the years ahead, Vision 2000 believes that it is important to stress the nature of the challenges that boards of governors are facing.

Under the changes we recommend, local boards would continue to be responsible and accountable for the general well-being of the colleges. The people who sit on local boards — those appointed from within the colleges and those drawn from the wider community — are part of the communities the colleges serve. They are aware of the local environment; they are in the best position to hear the voices of those whose needs the colleges seek to meet; and they can evaluate on a first-hand basis the impact of policy initiatives on their institution.

Boards would have increased and clarified responsibilities under the renewal initiatives we propose in this report. Their commitment to change will be fundamental to the success of any new directions. Their support for the renewed mandate that Vision 2000 proposes will be essential for that mandate to have meaning and practical expression throughout the system.

Local boards can help encourage and support the evolution of a "system of colleges" into a "college system." A true college system will be composed of 23 interdependent institutions responding to local and regional needs in highly individualized ways, but held together by a common mandate, core values about students and other clients, and collective beliefs about self-renewal and innovation.

To assure quality on a system-wide basis, we have recommended in Chapter 4 the establishment of system-wide standards and regular program review, under the auspices of a new College Standards and Accreditation Council (CSAC). This would require boards to participate in program reviews, conducted under the auspices of CSAC, using mainly external evaluators, and to develop and implement necessary responses to the results of program reviews.

However, the responsibilities in programming that boards now have would be largely unaffected by CSAC. Boards would continue to:

- determine their own mix of program offerings;
- develop proposals for new programs;
- decide the specific content and delivery form of all credential programs;
- be responsible for the updating of resources (capital, human and curricular);
- develop initiatives to meet provincial and sectoral needs, working in co-operation with other institutions; and
- provide, within the guidelines for fee-for-service training, contract training to employers and governments.

Boards would also continue to seek advice from local program advisory committees, college councils (which advise the college president and include a variety of stakeholders from the internal college community), administration, faculty, staff, community groups, and other stakeholders.

Under the proposals in this report, boards should have more valuable information with which to analyze and evaluate college operations. For example, the Strategic Planning Committee, recommended in Chapter 7, would provide an annual report to the Minister and to each college board of governors and council. The committee, to be set up under COR, would analyze and offer advice on major issues related to quality, access and funding in the college system.

This provincial planning committee would also co-ordinate information and plans for the sharing of specialized resources, another area in which local boards would carry the initiative. The co-operation and support of local boards are necessary if more intra-system sharing is to become a reality.

In Chapter 5, we emphasized the importance of increasing participation by those groups who have been traditionally underserved. We offer a definition of educational equity which highlights the need to remove systemic barriers to educational opportunities for such groups as women, visible minorities, aboriginal peoples, persons with disabilities and people living in poverty. Vision 2000 asks boards to ensure that they have in place:

- educational equity policies and formally defined measures for implementing and monitoring those policies;
- race and ethnic relations policies to promote tolerance and understanding;
- mechanisms to monitor employment equity; and
- mechanisms for building and maintaining effective partnerships with special communities and for advocating on their behalf on issues of educational equity.

Here again, the commitment of local boards will be crucial to making real progress. Boards are charged, for example, with seeing that college personnel, committees and other internal bodies are reflective of the diverse communities the colleges serve. (COR needs to ensure that the boards themselves reflect the communities they serve.) We have left to the discretion of the boards how they choose to implement and monitor these directions. We expect that some boards will appoint special advisory groups in the colleges to track progress on equity issues or to reach out to special communities. Whatever the methods boards choose to pursue these directions, we have recommended that they include a section on "serving communities" in their annual report to the Minister.

College boards are also urged to develop strategies for establishing long-term relationships with local fee-for-service clients, such as employers and governments.

We expect boards to be responsible for increasing opportunities for student success. We assume that colleges will:

- conduct assessments of literacy and numeracy levels of applicants to credential programs for the purposes of appropriate placement;
- provide preparatory courses for post-secondary students who require extra help;
- continue to provide basic education programs for adults; and
- improve programs and services for adult part-time learners through such methods as more flexible hours, modes and locations of instruction.

An educational system that remains highly compartmentalized will become less and less effective. College boards must work with other colleges, and with schools and universities to remove institutional barriers to student mobility throughout the educational system. In addition to recommendations in Chapter 6 related to improving school-college-university links at the local and provincial levels, college boards might try co-operative ventures with other educational bodies on continuing education and literacy programs. College boards might also take an active role in fostering cross-appointments with other educational institutions in order to facilitate co-operation and sharing of information and resources.

Boards of governors also have a vital role to play in the development of the human resources, curriculum and delivery methods of the colleges. In Chapter 8, we discuss the need for boards to set budgetary targets and policy guidelines for human resource development, and to report annually to the Minister on their progress in implementing them. Boards are also urged to foster applied scholarship in their colleges as a way of enhancing the primacy of the teaching function. Furthermore, they should develop constructive methods of performance review for all employees.

The curriculum and delivery objectives of Vision 2000 should influence the criteria used in the hiring of college personnel. We anticipate that, due to retirements, there will be a significant number of vacancies in the years ahead. Hiring for teacher excellence, as defined by the renewed mandate, should be an important component of the system's overall human resource planning process.

The renewed mandate says that colleges should strive to be model employers in the manner in which they invest in and manage human resource development, in their commitment to equity and in the creation of a positive, healthy and supportive working environment. Boards of governors should be responsible for behaving as exemplary employers in their communities.

The mandate also defines colleges as participatory institutions in which decision-making involves both internal and external stakeholders. That means that college boards should be looking to employers and labour, alumni and students, representatives of community groups and governments, as well as administration, faculty and support staff for their counsel in making decisions.

College boards will need the support, advice and enthusiasm of a range of stakeholders to help with the renewal of the system for the 21st century. Boards will also have to plan strategically, and make the best use of available data on such issues as quality, access and funding.

 Recommendation 38

> **Each college's board of governors should further develop its capacity for strategic planning, especially those issues related to quality, access and funding, and for working in partnership with a range of stakeholders to meet student needs.**

9.3 The Role of the Ontario Council of Regents

Over the past several years, the role of COR has been changing. Historically, the Council has had responsibilities in such areas as program approval, collective bargaining, and appointing members to the colleges' boards of governors. In 1986, the Pitman report recommended that the Minister establish an advisory council on colleges to undertake long-range planning.[68] In 1987, COR entered a period of transition, moving increasingly into a planning and policy advisory role, with responsibilities related to program approval shifting to the Ministry of Colleges and Universities

---

[68] Walter Pitman, *The Report of the Advisor to the Minister of Colleges and Universities on the Governance of the Colleges of Applied Arts and Technology* (Toronto: Ministry of Colleges and Universities, June 1986), p. 29.

(MCU). In 1988, the Gandz report recommended that COR yield its collective bargaining responsibilities to an employers' association.[69] And in 1989, MCU indicated the government's intention to move in this direction.

Divestment of the collective bargaining role will assist COR in working collaboratively with the full range of stakeholders in the college system, including the Ontario Public Service Employees Union. However, it has taken more time than expected for COR to make the transition from an agent for collective bargaining to a strategic planning body. While Vision 2000 is an example of collaborative planning that was conducted under the umbrella of the Council's new role, the process was interrupted by a faculty strike in the fall of 1989. This labour dispute further underlined the incompatibility between these two distinct roles of COR.

In anticipation of COR being relieved of its collective bargaining role, Vision 2000 has recommended that the Council assume responsibility for:

- CSAC, which would oversee the development of system-wide standards and program reviews; it would be "independently associated" with COR as a freestanding body;

- the Strategic Planning Committee for the college system, which would be a standing committee of COR; the Committee would be one means by which COR would fulfil its long-term planning and advisory functions; it would also provide information and analyses to important stakeholder groups such as the Association of Colleges of Applied Arts and Technology and its councils;

- developing system-wide guidelines to assist colleges in developing educational equity policies; and providing an annual public report on initiatives of the colleges in "serving communities" in the areas of educational equity, race and ethnic relations, employment equity and community partnerships;

- establishing an ad hoc task force to examine fee-for-service training issues ;

- working, under the Ministry's leadership, with universities and colleges, and other groups to create a new provincial institute "without walls" for advanced training; and

- engaging in other joint activities with planning and policy bodies; for example, numerous benefits could be realized if COR and the Ontario Council on University Affairs, where relevant and appropriate, established a closer working relationship.

Initially, we considered creating new entities to carry on many of these functions. However, we decided to vest them in the Council for three reasons. First, we wished to avoid a proliferation of new "bodies" and accompanying bureaucracies; second, COR has some valuable expertise and is a recognized and functioning part of the system now; and third, Vision 2000 hopes that COR can expand on the goodwill and collaboration that has characterized the Vision 2000 process.

One of the important current roles of COR is appointing members of college boards of governors. The current process for appointing external members should be strengthened to ensure that local boards have the requisite capabilities to provide the leadership that will be needed in the coming decades. Board members must be representative of the local communities that they serve, and boards

---

69 Colleges Collective Bargaining Commission, *The Report of Colleges Collective Bargaining Commission* (Toronto: Ontario Ministry of Colleges and Universities, January 1988), p. 179.

must have the resident experience and expertise required for the challenges ahead. Vision 2000 believes that COR should continue to improve the process for the selection of external members for the college boards.

 Recommendation 39

The Council of Regents should conduct an operational review of its board appointment responsibilities, employing a third-party process.

In this review, COR should consider ways to help boards draw upon the widest possible source of potential competent nominees and to develop relationships with key partner groups in the community, such as employers, labour, school boards, universities, and social agencies. The review should encourage local boards to provide advice to COR about its role in board appointments.

Vision 2000 believes that the responsibilities we have outlined for COR will strengthen its capacity to provide the Minister with independent and valuable policy advice and enable it to assist the colleges as they embark on new directions.

10

Starting Points for Change

10.1 Preamble

Vision 2000 has sought to achieve the complementary goals of developing a clear sense of direction for the colleges and forging a consensus about that direction through a collaborative process involving a broad range of constituencies. The process itself has been a milestone for the Ontario college system, and we hope it has set in motion a new era of collaboration and co-operation. For Vision 2000, the process has proven to be an important part of the product.

This report was made possible by the hundreds of people who freely gave their time, energy and ideas to our investigation. Vision 2000 has enabled some new partnerships to form and some old ones to be rekindled. What is necessary within colleges, across the system and beyond, is that these partnerships be strengthened and extended. As the process enters the next phase — that of further evaluation and implementation — the continued nurturing of these partnerships is perhaps even more essential. An environment which encourages involvement will help ensure system-wide commitment to the renewed mandate and an ongoing capability to develop our vision for the future.

We believe it is vitally important that all stakeholders, both inside and outside the college system, have an early opportunity to understand and respond to the directions and recommendations in this report. We also believe it is essential that key partners should be involved in any implementation process that the Minister might set in motion.

Vision 2000's agenda was established by the college system's internal and external stakeholders. Our report reflects the concerns and aspirations which the many constituencies hold to be most central and salient to the system's future. This report is not, nor does it claim to be, an exhaustive examination of every issue and policy of concern to the colleges.

An example of an issue which did not achieve prominence during our consultative process is that of college catchment areas or geographic boundaries. These boundaries, set at the inception of the colleges, were intended to define the area in which a college could offer its programs. Although these boundaries are perhaps an outmoded feature of the college system, they were not identified as an issue of pressing concern by the constituencies Vision 2000 consulted.

Other issues not addressed in this report may well be the focus of further assessment. In fact, we urge that the process of renewal continue. Good strategic planning and policy development can never wait until a snapshot has been taken of every item, but must work in a dynamic fashion to integrate new information, issues and ideas over time.

We hope that the Council of Regents (COR) and college constituencies interested in strategic planning, policy development and implementation will continue to build upon the ideas and visions that were submitted to us.

10.2 Taking the Next Step

Implementation of Vision 2000's recommendations will depend on harnessing both the knowledge of the key stakeholders and their commitment to the realization of the renewed mandate. It is the full range of stakeholders, from the Ministry of Colleges and Universities (MCU) and college faculty and staff to students and the community, who will be called upon to put the mandate into practice. They are the ones most familiar with the relevant data and workable alternative models for implementation. They are the ones who must take the next steps.

We fully recognize the responsibilities of Vision 2000's sponsoring ministry, MCU, with respect to implementation of public policy. It has been our understanding from the outset that our task was to advise on direction and strategies on "how to get there from here." But it remains government's role to provide leadership in co-ordinating discussions and developing the more detailed action plans necessary to realize those Vision 2000 goals which the government supports.

 Recommendation 40

The Minister of Colleges and Universities should establish a Vision 2000 Implementation Committee to co-ordinate evaluation and development of detailed plans for implementation of Vision 2000's recommendations. This committee should involve all of the major constituencies, both internal and external, that participated in Vision 2000.

In order to sustain the co-operative impetus of Vision 2000 and gather the important insights provided by different constituencies, the membership of this committee should include representation from the Council of Presidents, college boards of governors, faculty, administration, students, support staff, the school system, the Ministry of Education, MCU, the Ontario Council of University Affairs, COR, and external stakeholders such as employers, labour and community groups. College system participation remains critical because those who work in the colleges are uniquely qualified to evaluate the direct and indirect costs of various innovations and recommendations and can ensure that good ideas for redirecting existing dollars, as well as important reasons for the provision of new funds, will be part of the implementation discussions. The Committee should be chaired by the Deputy Minister of MCU.

The Committee's task should involve the determination of which recommendations:

- are at the top of the implementation timetable;
- warrant experimentation before full-scale implementation;
- require that new legislation be drafted;
- require new funding;
- necessitate a redirection of funds; and
- require further consultation and research.

10.3 Considering Costs and Benefits

Assessing the costs and benefits associated with a series of recommendations such as those put forward in this report is always a difficult task. Both the identification and quantification of the costs and benefits of a renewed mandate will depend upon a variety of assumptions and circumstances.

First, a wide range of macro-economic and social trends such as employment levels, immigration and labour force participation rates play central roles in determining the costs and benefits of college education. Second, choices among different administrative and organizational models may generate significantly different cost/benefit structures. The renewed mandate envisions new ways of reaching the goals of the college system; new partnerships are expected to change the costs and benefits generated by colleges. Finally, a full cost/benefit analysis must attempt to take into account factors such as the opportunity costs related to the forgone earnings of students, excessive search time by employers looking for workers with the right skills, devalued educational achievement when credits earned in one institution are not recognized by another institution and other real costs which defy simple quantification.

To a certain extent, the most significant issue for decision-makers is the cost of not proceeding with a renewal of the colleges' mandate. If Ontario does not take major steps to reinvigorate the colleges, we believe that there will be serious economic and social costs. These costs include those associated with: an inadequate skill base to meet the needs of the economy; the underutilization of students' prior educational investments due to inadequate links between colleges, schools, and universities and the lack of credit for prior learning; failed partnerships and missed opportunities due to inadequate planning and co-ordination, including the costs to employers of attempting to co-ordinate their needs at a sectoral level with the colleges; continued duplication of quality control efforts as each college works in relative isolation; a lack of clear paths for access; and inappropriate curricula for workers in need of retraining.

We believe there will be significant economic and social benefits associated with the renewed mandate that we have proposed for the colleges. In addition to avoiding the types of costs identified above, implementing the renewed mandate would provide benefits such as: improved prestige for colleges as quality is assured; greater likelihood that students will choose career education; progress toward redressing income and skill polarization through greater educational equity and increased access; citizens who are more knowledgeable about the society in which they live; and better morale and confidence in the college system.

Renewing the colleges' mandate will likely entail some additional investment in the system. Per-student instructional costs of college programs may increase; some of the costs associated with administering the system may rise; and enrolment will likely be higher than would have otherwise been the case. However, these increases should not be inordinate as there are also savings and efficiencies associated with implementing the measures we have proposed.

For example, if there are increases in instructional costs due to increases in the generic and general education content of college programs, they would be incrementally phased in and could, in part, be offset by reductions in the costs associated with specific skills training and methods of curriculum delivery. Similarly, additional investment in student assessment and placement, and preparatory courses may yield efficiencies by allowing post-secondary instruction to take place in more academically homogeneous classes composed of better-prepared students than is currently the case. In addition, while total instructional costs would not decline, these initiatives will help lower student attrition rates and should result in lower expenditures per graduate.

Among the administrative costs of implementing our proposals are those associated with the development of program standards and ongoing, system-wide program review. Although establishing CSAC and its program councils to oversee these activities entails costs, some of these costs are already borne by both the colleges and many groups external to the system. Included here are the costs of individual colleges' efforts to establish standards and review programs. In addition, the costs of evaluation to both individual employers and professional associations would likely be reduced considerably by their involvement in CSAC.

Increased enrolment in college programs will require additional investment in the college system. However, in addition to the savings accruing to industry from having a more highly — and appropriately — trained workforce, we would expect that more equitable access would result in savings in other areas of government social expenditures. For example, the benefits to the taxpayer, as well as to individuals, business, and the community as a whole, of increased funding for adult basic education programs have been noted in a myriad of reports.

As the preceding discussion indicates, the quantification of the costs and benefits of our proposals for renewing the college system's mandate is a complex problem. There will always be some uncertainty about the exact magnitude of the costs and benefits. We are confident, however, that the social return on the investments required for the renewal of the college system's mandate will be competitive with returns on other successful public investments. The college system, given the appropriate support to achieve the goals we have set for it, should contribute much to the future well-being of Ontario's citizens.

10.4 Beyond Vision 2000: Progress through Partnerships

Some of Vision 2000's recommendations will be easy to implement in a relatively short time frame. For instance, COR should be able to quickly establish a strategic planning committee which will be able to produce a sequel to Vision 2000's environmental scan, *With the Future in Mind: 1991.* On the other hand, realizing the full benefits of a broadened curriculum, consistent standards and a quality-assurance body made up of internal and external stakeholders will take considerably longer. These initiatives will require the continued nurturing of partnerships and a series of clearly defined interim steps.

Our hope is that Vision 2000's most important legacy will be a new way of doing business for the colleges, one centred on renewed respect for both internal and external partners and the need for the college system to listen actively to employers, labour, communities, governments and colleagues in other parts of the educational spectrum. As well, the future should include a renewed sense of confidence for the colleges.

The colleges' ability to be effective partners must begin at home, with strong and healthy working relationships within each college and across the system. Vision 2000 has rediscovered the extraordinary creativity and collaboration resident in the system. We have received briefs and visions from hundreds of ad hoc groups and newly formed coalitions, as well as many important traditional constituencies. Vision 2000 has provided an opportunity to recognize and build upon past and current successes as a way of preparing for a different and challenging future.

Preparing for the future will require many changes, not just for Ontario's colleges. The colleges have a crucial role to play in assisting Ontario to adapt and succeed in a new economic and social reality. But in order to be effective instruments of public policy, the government must begin to include the colleges, from the outset of the policy process, as major partners in provincial planning. We believe that, taken together, our recommendations indicate why an integrated, co-ordinated and collaborative approach to shaping policies for the future is necessary. The colleges are, in our estimation, ready to take on the tasks and engage in the needed partnerships. We hope they will be invited to do so.

To call this the "final" report of Vision 2000 is inconsistent with the major intent of the process. We hope that this document, as the latest report about the college system, will contribute to the ongoing process of developing a renewed capability and commitment to thinking and acting strategically together.

APPENDICES

Members of Vision 2000 Study Teams

Members of Study Team 1

Robert Bernhardt,
Formerly Director of Planning,
Sheridan College

Ron Chopowick,
Director, Academic Services,
Association of Colleges of Applied Arts and
  Technology of Ontario

Ron Golemba,
Professor
Centennial College

Drew Nameth,
Manager,
Financial Support Unit,
Ministry of Colleges and Universities

Michel Parent,
Administrator, French Language Services,
Niagara College

Robert Struthers,
Dean,
Continuing Education and Marketing,
George Brown College

Ralph Wood,
Professor,
Sir Sandford Fleming College

Helen Burstyn,
Deputy Secretary,
Premier's Council Secretariat
Government of Ontario

Peter Dawson,
Member,
Ontario Council of Regents, and
President, Dawson Group

Jim C. Hsu,
Senior Analyst,
Labour Market Research,
Ministry of Skills Development

Karen O'Kaln,
Senior Policy Advisor,
Research Support & International Activities Branch,
Ministry of Colleges and Universities

Howard Rundle (Chair),
Vice-President, Academic,
Fanshawe College

Brian Wolfe, (Executive Officer),
Senior Policy Analyst,
Ontario Council of Regents

Herb Young,
Former President,
Loyalist College

Members of Study Team 2

Hugh Armstrong,
Associate Dean, General Studies,
Centennial College

André Bekerman,
Senior Negotiator,
Ontario Public Service Employees Union

Gordon Betcherman,
Project Director, Employment,
Economic Council of Canada

Kris Gataveckas,
Vice-President of Development,
Humber College

John Huot,
President, Faculty Union, Local 562,
Ontario Public Service Employees Union, and
Professor, Humber College

Louis Lizotte,
Senior Analyst, French Language Services Section,
Ministry of Colleges and Universities

Hugh Mackenzie,
Research Director,
United Steel Workers of America

Janet Mason,
Manager, Policy and Planning Branch,
Ministry of Skills Development

Riel Miller, (Executive Officer),
Manager, Policy and Research,
Ontario Council of Regents

Milton Orris,
Dean, Continuing Education Division,
Ryerson Polytechnical Institute

Jacqueline Robertson,
Director, Services Section,
La Cité collégiale

Tayce Wakefield,
Manager, Government Relations Staff,
General Motors of Canada Ltd.

David Wolfe,
Associate Professor, Department of Political Science,
University of Toronto

Robert Arn,
President,
Educational Software Products,

Jim Bennett,
Vice-President and General Manager,
Canadian Federation of Independent Business

Sandford Borins,
Professor, School of Administrative Studies,
York University

Sam Gindin,
Special Assistant to the President,
Canadian Auto Workers

Steve Krar,
Consultant,
Kelmar Associates

Mike Lyons,
President,
Impact Labour Representatives

Lorna Marsden, (Chair),
Professor, Department of Sociology,
University of Toronto, and
Senator, Toronto-Taddle Creek

Ron McGinley,
Director, Demographics and Social Economics Branch,
Ministry of Treasury and Economics

Neil Nelson,
Management Consultant, and
Past President, Ontario Society for Training and
    Development

Gary Polonsky,
President,
Durham College

Susie Vallance,
Regional Vice-President, OPSEU, and
Education Employment Equity Officer, Seneca College

Peter Warrian,
Executive Director,
Canadian Steel Trade and Employment Congress

Past Member:
Pierre LeBlanc
Senior Analyst, French Language Services Section,
Ministry of Colleges and Universities

Members of Study Team 3

Francie Aspinall, (Executive Officer),
Professor,
Department of English
Centennial College

Carol Brooks,
Vice-Chair, Social Assistance Review Board,
Ministry of Community & Social Services

Ruth Gates, (Chair)
Vice-President, Community Services,
Fanshawe College

Sharon Goldberg,
Supervisor, Continuing Education Conference Centre,
Sir Sandford Fleming College

Wilson Head,
Past President,
Urban Alliance for Race Relations, and
Retired Professor, York University

Maureen Hynes,
Multicultural Co-ordinator,
Community Outreach Department,
George Brown College

Carolle C.-Laflamme,
Regional Field Worker
Direction-Jeunesse

Jill Morgan,
Ontario Public Service Employees Union Negotiator,,
and Employment Counsellor, Futures Program,
St. Clair College

Bev Turner,
Vice-President, Access Programs,
Durham College

Philomen Wright,
Member,
Ontario Rent Review Board, and
Past Member, Ontario Council of Regents

Bernice Bell,
Professor,
College Vocational Program,
Seneca College

Gordon Cressy,
Vice-President,
Development & University Relations,
University of Toronto

Louise Eaton,
Special Needs Co-ordinator,
Cambrian College

Jim Griffis,
Member of the
Ontario Council of Regents

Patty Holmes,
Former Vice-Chair,
Canadian Association of Independent Living Centres

Jane Kirkwood,
Chief Analyst,
Commercial & Operational Services,
Ministry of Colleges & Universities

Valerie McGregor,
Director,
Aboriginal Post-Secondary Counselling Unit

Dave Robertson,
College Special Needs Consultant,
Centennial College,
Warden Woods Campus

Brenda Wall,
Project Director,
Metro Labour Education Centre

Steve Zerebny,
Program Co-ordinator,
Apprenticeship Branch,
Ministry of Skills Development

Members of Study Team 4

George Allan,
Professor,
Departments of Mathematics and Instrumentation,
Lambton College

Maureen Dey,
Chair,
English Department,
Seneca College

Harv Honsberger, (Executive Officer),
Director,
Instructional and Human Resource Development,
Sheridan College

Jay Jackson,
President, Local 245, Ontario Public Service Employees
    Union, and
Technologist, Faculty of Visual Arts, Sheridan College

Frank Lockington,
Co-ordinator,
Ontario Skills Development Office,
St. Lawrence College

Keith McIntyre, (Chair),
President,
Mohawk College

Norman Rowen,
Research Consultant

Adam Sugden,
Co-ordinator of Pulp & Paper Engineering Program,
Sault College

Helmut Zisser,
General Manager,
Federal/Provincial Relations,
Ministry of Skills Development

Terry Dance,
Dean,
Access & Program Development,
George Brown College

Roy Giroux,
Vice-President,
Education & Faculty Services,
Humber College

Garth Jackson,
Vice-President,
Academic,
George Brown College

Bill Kuehnbaum,
President Local 655, Ontario Public Service Employees
    Union, and
Professor, Cambrian College

Richard Marleau,
Professor, School of Business,
Canadore College

Pat McNeil,
Manager, Beach Tree Cafe, and
Graduate of Centennial College & York University

Karen Shaw,
Executive Director,
Cambrian Foundation,
Cambrian College

Bill Summers,
Manager,
Program Services,
Ministry of Colleges & Universities

Past member:
Fran Lacey
Registrar,
Algonquin College

Members of Study Team 5

Eileen Burrows,
Professor,
Health Sciences,
Centennial College

Bill Conrod,
Vice-President Continuing Education,
Algonquin College

Diane Crocker,
University Affairs Officer,
University Relations Branch,
Ministry of Colleges and Universities

Brian Desbiens,
President,
Sir Sandford Fleming College

Mark Larratt-Smith,
Assistant Deputy Minister,
Ministry of Education

Ian McLellan,
Supervising Principal,
Community Development Branch,
North York Board of Education

Edward J. Monahan,
Executive Director,
Council of Ontario Universities

Penny Moss, (Chair),
Executive Director,
Ontario Public School Boards Association

Jo Oppenheimer,
Research Consultant,
Oppenheimer Research Associates

Brenda Protheroe,
Supervising Principal Continuing Education,
City of York, Board of Education

Jim Turk,
Director of Education,
Ontario Federation of Labour

Past Member:
Barry Pervin
Senior Policy Advisor,
Policy and Planning Branch,
Ministry of Skills Development

Diane Chevalier,
Acting Director, French-Media,
Algonquin College

Felicity Corelli,
Research Consultant

Susan Davey,
Principal,
Bickford Park High School

Terence Grier,
President,
Ryerson Polytechnical Institute

Bert Martin,
President,
St. Clair College

Vicki Milligan,
Chair,
Articulation/High School Liaison,
Seneca College

Desmond Morton,
Principal, Erindale College,
University of Toronto

Starr Olsen, (Executive Officer),
Consultant, Professional Development,
Humber College

George Pedersen,
President,
University of Western Ontario

Peter Stokes,
Analyst,
Commercial Services Unit,
Ministry of Colleges & Universities

Scott Turner,
Dean, School of Visual Arts,
Sheridan College

Members of Sixth Table

Alfred Abouchard,
Superintendent, Ottawa-Carlton French Language
School Board,
President, Association multiculturelle francophone,
and
Member, CEFO

Louise Eaton,
Representative from
Study Team 3

Carolle C.-Laflamme,
Representative from
Study Team 3

Richard Marleau,
Representative from
Study Team 4

Maurice Perrier, (Committee Chair)
Professor, Northern College, and
Member, CEFO

Jacqueline Robertson,
Representative from
Study Team 2

Diane Chevalier,
Representative from
Study Team 5

Marc Godbout,
Representative from
Steering Committee

Andreé Lortie,
President,
La Cité collégiale, and
Member, CEFO

Michel Parent
Representative from
Study Team 1

Lionel Poirier,
Executive Co-ordinator, Francophone Affairs,
Ministry of Colleges and Universities

Nicole Vigeant,
Manager,
French Language Services Section,
Ministry of Colleges and Universities

B

Vision 2000 Co-ordinators

The following individuals served as Vision 2000 Co-ordinators for the colleges. Co-ordinators served as a liaison between the Vision 2000 research secretariat and the colleges. Their task was to encourage their college's participation in the review process and keep their college informed as to the progress of the study. The Steering Committee wishes to express its appreciation to these individuals who gave of their time and expertise to Vision 2000.

Algonquin College
Robin Dorrell,
Director,
Marketing & Public Affairs

Cambrian College
Linda Wilson,
Director of Public Affairs,

Glenys Lafrance,
Assistant to the President

Canadore College
Michael Manson,
Assistant to the President

Centennial College
Margaret Kende,
Executive Director,
Strategic Marketing & Planning

Conestoga College
Larry Rechsteiner,
Associate Director,
Long Range Planning

Confederation College
Jean Bujold,
Marketing Officer,
     Community Relations,

Robert Mitchelson,
Vice-President, Administration

Durham College
Bonnie Ginter-Brown,
Chair, Nursing Diploma Program

Fanshawe College
Emily Marcoccia,
Manager, Public Relations

George Brown College
Bob Struthers,
Dean, Marketing & Continuing Education

Georgian College
Fred Ruemper,
Professor, School of Business, and
     Chair, College Council

Humber College

Bev Walden,
Associate Dean of Planning, and

Michael Harper,
Dean, Technology

Lambton College

George Allan,
Professor,
Departments of Mathematics, and
Instrumentation & Control

Mohawk College

Andy Tapajna,
Director, College Planning

Northern College

Theresa Savord,
Administrative Assistant,
Student Services Department,

Phillipe Boissonneault,
Principal, Kapuskasing Campus

Seneca College

Tony Tilly,
Dean, Continuing Education

Sir Sandford Fleming College

Paul Smith,
Director of Planning & Staff Development,

Margaret Dickson,
Acting Director, Planning and Special Projects

St. Lawrence College

Robin Pepper,
Director of Communications

La Cité collégiale

Lucien Courbin,
Assistant to the President

Loyalist College

Maureen Piercy,
Director, Community Affairs

Niagara College

George Repar,
Director, Planning, Research & Development

Sault College

Penny Gardiner,
Chair, Academic Services

Sheridan College

Lynne Mulder,
Dean, Health Sciences,

Bob Bernhardt,
Former Director of Planning

St. Clair College

Lynn Watts,
Director,
Planning & Budget

C

Vision 2000 Background Papers

Background papers prepared for Study Team 1

The Determinants of Enrolment Rates and Enrolments in Ontario Community Colleges
David K. Foot and Maia MacNiven

The College System — An Empirical Snapshot
Vision 2000

With the Future in Mind: An Environmental Scan
Vision 2000

Background papers prepared for Study Team 2:

Choosing Equity and Prosperity: Access to College and the Ontario Economy
Pat Armstrong and Hugh Armstrong

Meeting the Competitive Challenge: Enhancing Applied Research in Ontario's Colleges
Sandford Borins and Shirley Holloway

Role of the Colleges in the Changing Economy — Report on Consultations
Audrey Gill

Toward a Highly Qualified Workforce: Improving the Terms of the Equity-Efficiency Trade-off
Rianne Mahon

Industrial Restructuring, Occupational Shifts and Skills: The Steel and Electronic Manufacturing Cases
Peter Warrian

New Technology and Education: A Challenge for the Colleges
David Wolfe

Background papers prepared for Study Team 3:

Meeting the Needs of Diverse Learners: Submissions from Community Organizations and the Colleges
Francie Aspinall

Post Secondary Skills Training and Education for Senior Citizens
Bernice Bell

Special Needs Students: Toward the Year 2000
Elizabeth Thorsen

Ontario's Community Colleges: Values for the Year 2000
Susan Wismer

Towards the Year 2000: Communities within Colleges
Susan Wismer

Relevancy and Linkages: Colleges and Communities Working Together
Susan Wismer

Background papers prepared for Study Team 4:

Alternative Delivery of Instruction in Post-Compulsory Education
George Allan

Access and Quality: Preparatory and Remedial Education in the Colleges
Terry Dance and Roy Giroux

Quality From an Instructional Perspective
Harv Honsberger

Tasks and Roles in Curriculum Development
Harv Honsberger

Themes and Implications: A Report on the Visions from the College System
Harv Honsberger

Expanding the Core: General Education, Generic Skills, and Core Curriculum in Ontario Community Colleges
Michael Park

Mini Scanning the Future
Irene Ross

Most Things to More People
Norman Rowen

Pressures for Change, Opportunities for Development
Norman Rowen

Towards a Self-Governing System: Some Aspects of Quality and Proposals for Change
Norman Rowen

Visions of Educational Technology in the Year 2000
John Taylor

◤ Background papers prepared for Study Team 5:

Summary of Submissions Received in Response to "An Invitation to Participate"
Felicity Corelli

College to University—An Analysis of Transfer Credit Policy and Practice
John Dennison

College-University Transfer Arrangements Existing in Ontario
Robert Alexander Marshall

Consultations on College-University Linkages
Craig McFadyen

The Relationship Between Schools and Colleges
Jo Oppenheimer

How Ontario's Colleges Might Respond to Pressures for the Provision of More Advanced Training
Michael Skolnik

Skilled and Educated: A Solution to Ontario's Urgent Need for More Polytechnic Programs
Stuart Smith

College Transfer Revisited: A Working Paper
Peter Stokes

◤ Other background papers prepared for Vision 2000:

Perceptions of the Colleges of Applied Arts and Technology: Interviews with Cabinet Ministers and Other MPPs
Peter Adams, Charles Pascal and Mora Thompson

Colleges in and of their Communities: A Case Study of Sault College, Elliot Lake Campus
Hugh Armstrong and Peter Warrian

Vision Franco-Ontarienne de l'avenir des collèges (Franco-Ontarian Vision of the Future of Colleges)
Anne Gilbert

Models for Increased Private Sector Financing of Training and Labour Market Development
Craig McFadyen and Robert Alexander Marshall

Vision 2000 Alumni Focus Group Summary Report
Charles Pascal

A Framework for Reviewing the Mandate of Ontario's System of Colleges of Applied Arts and Technology
Vision 2000

D

Selected Bibliography

Advisory Council on Adjustment, *Adjusting to Win*, Report of the [de Grandpre] Advisory Council on Adjustment (Ottawa: Supply and Services Canada, 1989)

Anisef, Paul, Frederick D. Ashbury, and Anton H. Turrittin, "Educational Diversity and Occupational Attainment: Are Community Colleges Fulfilling their Promise?" (Paper presented at the Learned Societies Conference, University of Laval, Quebec City, June 4, 1989)

Asinef, Paul, *Career Community College Students in Canada, A Decade of Change: An Analysis of the 1974/75 and 1983/84 Post-secondary Student Surveys* (North York, Ontario: York University, 1988)

Association of Canadian Community Colleges, *Literacy in the Colleges and Institutes* (1989)

Astin, Alexander W., *Achieving Educational Excellence: A Critical Assessment of Priorities and Practices in Higher Education* (San Francisco: Jossey-Bass, 1987)

Blaug, Mark, "Where are We Now in the Economics of Education?" *Economics of Education Review*, Vol. 4, No. 1, (1985), pp. 17-28

Bowen, Howard R., *The Costs of Higher Education — How Much Do Colleges and Universities Spend per Student and How Much Should They Spend?* (San Francisco, Jossey-Bass, 1980)

Brundtland, Gro, *Our Common Future: The World Commission on Environment and Development* (Oxford: Oxford University Press, 1987)

Canada Employment and Immigration Advisory Council, *Older Workers: An Imminent Crisis in the Labour Market* (Ottawa: CEIC, August 1985)

Canada Employment and Immigration Advisory Council, *The Unemployed Older Worker Phenomenon: A Problem That Will Not Go Away* (Ottawa: CEIC, June 1988)

Canadian Labour Market and Productivity Centre, "The Changing Nature of the Canadian Labour Market: The Increased Importance of Education and Training," *Quarterly Labour Market and Productivity Review* (Winter 1988)

Cantor, Leonard, "Public Sector Higher Education, 1945-1986," in W. A. C. Stewart (ed.), *Higher Education in Postwar Britain* (London: MacMillan, 1989), pp. 296-313

CEDEFOP, *Vocational Training Systems in the Member States of the European Community, A Comparative Study* (Berlin: European Centre for the Development of Vocational Training, 1984)

College Committee on International Education, "International Education and the Ontario Colleges of Applied Arts & Technology" (Toronto: Ontario Ministry of Colleges and Universities, 1989)

Colleges Collective Bargaining Commission, *The Report of Colleges Collective Bargaining Commission* (Toronto: Ontario Ministry of Colleges and Universities, January 1988)

Colleges Committee on Academic Affairs and Ontario Secondary Schools Principals' Council, "The Development of Effective Liaison Between the Colleges of Applied Arts and Technology and the Public Secondary Schools of Ontario" (Toronto, November 1988)

Collins, Graham, "Ontario's Colleges of Applied Arts and Technology in the 1990s: An Agenda for Action" (Toronto: Association of Colleges of Applied Arts and Technology of Ontario, 1988)

Commission on Post-Secondary Education in Ontario, *The Learning Society* (Toronto: Ministry of Government Services, 1972)

Commission on the Future of Community Colleges, *Building Communities, A Vision for a New Century* (Washington, D.C.: American Association of Community and Junior Colleges, 1988)

Committee on Academic Affairs, "Student Retention/Attrition in Ontario CAATs" (South Porcupine, Ontario: Northern College, June 1989)

Confederation College, *The Barriers Project* (Thunder Bay, Ontario: Confederation College of Applied Arts and Technology, 1989)

Conrad, Clifton F. and Richard F. Wilson, *Academic Program Reviews: Institutional Approaches, Expectations and Controversies* (ASCH-ERIC Higher Education Reports, Number 5, 1985)

Creative Research Group, *Literacy in Canada: A Research Report* (a report prepared for Southam News, Ottawa, 1987)

Cross, K. Patricia, *Adults as Learners* (San Francisco: Jossey-Bass, 1986)

Davis, (The Honourable) William, *Statement in the Legislature* (May 21, 1965)

Dawkins, J. S. & A. C. Holding, *Skills for Australia* (Canberra: Australian Government Publishing Service, 1987)

Deloitte, Haskins & Sells, *The Funding of Vocational Education and Training, A Consultation Document* (London: Manpower Services Commission, 1988)

Dennison, John D. and Paul Gallagher, *Canada's Community Colleges: A Critical Analysis,* (Vancouver, 1986)

Dennison, John D. and John S. Levin, *Canada's Community Colleges in the 1980s* (Vancouver: University of British Columbia, August, 1988)

Dertouzos, Michael L., Richard K. Lester and Robert M. Solow, *Made in America: Regaining the Productive Edge,* The MIT Commission on Industrial Productivity (Cambridge, Massachusetts: MIT Press, 1989)

Dietsche, Peter, *Describing and Predicting Freshmen Attrition in a College of Applied Arts and Technology of Ontario,* (Unpublished Doctoral Thesis, O.I.S.E., University of Toronto, Toronto, 1988)

Dirrheimer, Angela, *Information Technology and the Training of Skilled Workers in the Service Sector* (Berlin: European Centre for the Development of Vocational Training, 1982)

Economic Council of Canada, *Innovation and Jobs in Canada* (Ottawa: Supply and Services Canada, 1987)

Economic Council of Canada, *Good Jobs, Bad Jobs, Employment in the Service Economy, A Statement by the Economic Council of Canada* (Ottawa: Ministry of Supply and Services, 1990)

Employment and Immigration Canada, *Employment Equity: A Guide for Employers* (Ottawa: Minister of Supply and Services, 1989)

Employment and Immigration Canada, *Success in the Works: A Profile of Canada's Emerging Workforce* (Ottawa: Minister of Supply and Services, 1989)

Employment and Immigration Canada, "The Levy/Grant Option," *Labour Market Development in the 1980s* (Ottawa: Minister of Supply and Services, 1981)

Employment and Immigration Canada, Skill Development Leave Task Force, *Learning a Living in Canada*, Vol. 1: Background and Perspectives (Ottawa: Supply and Services Canada, 1983)

Finegold, David & D. Sosckie, "The Failure of Training in Britain: Analysis and Prescription," *Oxford Review of Economic Policy* Vol. 4, No. 3 (Autumn, 1989), pp. 20-53

Fortin, Michele, *Accessibility to and Participation in the Post-Secondary Education System in Canada* (Saskatoon: National Forum on Post-Secondary Education, October 1987)

Freeman, Christopher, *Technology Policy and Economic Performance: Lessons from Japan* (London: Pinter Publishers, 1987)

George, Melvin D., "Assessing Program Quality," in (R. F. Wilson, editor) Designing Academic Program Reviews, *New Directions for Higher Education*, No. 37 (San Francisco: Jossey-Bass, 1982)

Heads of Language Executive, *Writing Across the College Resource Guide* (June, 1989)

Hynes, Maureen, *Access to Potential: A Two-Way Street, and Educational and Training Needs Assessment of Metro Toronto's Diverse Racial and Cultural Communities* (Toronto: George Brown College, 1987)

Hynes, Maureen, *Equity and Access Issues: Educational and Training Needs of Diverse Racial and Cultural Communities, or It Takes Time to Turn the Queen Mary Around* (Toronto: George Brown College, 1988)

Instructional Assignment Review Committee, *Survival or Excellence?* (Toronto: Ministry of Colleges and Universities, July 1985)

Jaccaci, August T., "The Social Architecture of a Learning Culture," *Training and Development Journal*, Vol. 43, No. 11, (November, 1989), p. 49-51

Joint Human Resources Committee, *Connections for the Future* (Toronto: Canadian Electrical and Electronic Manufacturing Industry, November, 1988)

Karolewski, Teresa, "Continuing Education in Ontario's Community Colleges: Student Profiles, Barriers and Exceptional Practices" (unpublished Vision 2000 paper, Toronto, 1989)

Knapper, Christopher K., George L. Geis, Charles E. Pascal and Bruce M. Shore, *If Teaching is Important: The evaluation of instruction in higher education* (Clarke, Irwin & Company Ltd., 1977)

Labour Canada, *Education and Working Canadians*, Report of the Commission of Inquiry on Educational Leave and Productivity (Ottawa: Minister of Supply and Services, 1979)

Le Conseil de l'education franco-ontarienne, *Plan directeur de l'education franco-ontarienne* (Toronto: CEFO, 1989)

Legave, C. & D. Vignaud, *Descriptions of the Vocational Training Systems — France* (Berlin: European Centre for the Development of Vocational Training, 1979)

Lemons, Dale C., *Education and Training for a Technological World* (Columbus Ohio: National Centre for Research in Vocational Education, Ohio State University, 1984)

Lewis, Anne M., *Descriptions of the Vocational Training System, United Kingdom* (Berlin: European Centre for the Development of Vocational Training, 1981)

Looking Ahead: Trends and Implications in the Social Environment (Toronto: Ontario Ministry of Community and Social Services, 1989)

Lowy, Louis and Darlene O'Connor, *Why Education in the Later Years?* (Lexington, Massachusetts: Lexington Books, 1986)

Marcus, Laurence R., Anita O. Leone and Edward D. Goldberg, *The Path to Excellence: Quality Assurance in Higher Education* (ASHE-ERIC Higher Education Research Report, Number 1, 1983)

McMillan, C. J., *Investing in Tomorrow: Japan's Science and Technology Organization and Strategies* (Ottawa: Canada-Japan Trade Council, 1989)

Miles, Ian, Howard Rush, Kevin Turner and John Bessant, *Information Horizons: The Long-Term Social Implications of New Information Technology* (Aldershot, Hants: Edward Elgar, 1988)

Ministry of Colleges and Universities (Ontario), *A Study of the Impact of OS:IS Implementation on the Post-Secondary System in Ontario* (Toronto: Ontario Ministry of Colleges and Universities, 1988)

Ministry of Colleges and Universities (Ontario), *Report of the Ontario Student Assistance Program 1986/87* (Thunder Bay: Ontario Ministry of Colleges and Universities, n.d.)

Ministry of Colleges and Universities (Ontario), *Accreditation Review Committee* (Draft Report, June 1989)

Ministry of Colleges and Universities (Ontario), "Provincial Program Standards" (Discussion Paper, April 1989)

Ministry of Colleges and Universities (Ontario), *Statistical Profile of Ontario Colleges of Applied Arts and Technology* (Toronto: Ontario Ministry of Colleges and Universities, 1989)

Ministry of Education/Ministry of Colleges and Universities (Ontario), *Secondary/Post-Secondary Interface Study* (Toronto: Ontario Ministry of Education/Ontario Ministry of Colleges and Universities, 1975)

Ministry of Education/Ministry of Colleges and Universities (Ontario), "Toward the Year 2000: Future Conditions and Strategic Options for the Support of Learning in Ontario," *Review and Evaluation Bulletin*, 5:1 (Toronto: Ontario Ministry of Education/Ontario Ministry of Colleges and Universities, 1984)

Ministry of Skills Development (Ontario), *Adjusting To Change: An Overview of Labour Market Issues* (Toronto: Ontario Ministry of Skills Development, June 1988)

Ministry of Skills Development, *Literacy — The Basics of Growth* (Toronto: Queen's Printer, 1988)

Ministry of Skills Development (Ontario), *Building a Training System For the 1990s: A Shared Responsibility* (Toronto: Ontario Ministry of Skills Development, February, 1989)

Munch, Joachim, *Vocational Training in the Federal Republic of Germany* (Berlin: European Centre for the Development of Vocational Training, 1982)

Muszynski, L., & D. Wolfe, "New Technology and Training: Lessons from Abroad," *Canadian Public Policy*, Vol. 15, No. 3 (1989), pp. 245-264

Noyelle, Thierry J., *Beyond Industrial Dualism: Market and Job Segmentation in the New Economy* (Boulder and London: Westview Press, 1987)

Oechslin, Jean-Jacques, "Training and the Business World: The French Experience," *International Labour Review*, Vol. 126, No. 6 (Nov-Dec, 1987), pp. 653-667

Office for Disabled Persons, *Statistical Profile of Disabled Persons in Ontario* (Toronto: Office for Disabled Persons, 1988)

Ontario Council on University Affairs, *What The Council Heard About Accessibility: The Ontario Dilemma* (Toronto: OCUA, 1990)

Ontario Department of Education, Colleges of Applied Arts and Technology, *Basic Documents* (Toronto: Ontario Department of Education, 1966)

Ontario Department of Education, Colleges of Applied Arts and Technology, *Basic Documents* (Toronto: Ontario Department of Education, 1967)

Ontario Manpower Commission, *Training in Industry: A Survey of Employer-Sponsored Programs in Ontario* (Toronto, 1986)

Ontario Senior Citizens Affairs, *A New Agenda: Health and Social Services Strategies for Ontario Senior Citizens* ([Toronto]: Minister for Senior Citizens' Affairs, March 1986)

Organisation for Economic Cooperation and Development, *New Technologies in the 1990s: A Socio-Economic Strategy*, Report of a Group of Experts on the Social Aspects of New Technologies (Paris: OECD, 1988)

Parnell, Dale, *The Neglected Majority* (Washington D.C.: The Community College Press; American Association of Community and Junior Colleges, 1985)

Pitman, Walter, *The Report of the Advisor to the Minister of Colleges and Universities on the Governance of the Colleges of Applied Arts and Technology* (Toronto: Ministry of Colleges and Universities, June 1986)

Porter, Marion and Gilles Jasmin, *A Profile of Post-Secondary Students in Canada* (Ottawa: Department of the Secretary of State for Canada, 1987)

Premier's Council (Ontario), *Competing in the New Global Economy*, Report of the Premier's Council, Vol. 1 (Toronto: Queen's Printer for Ontario, 1988)

Premier's Council (Ontario), *Competing in the New Global Economy*, Report of the Premier's Council, Industry Studies, Vol. 2 (Toronto: Queen's Printer for Ontario, 1988)

Premier's Council (Ontario), *Competing in the New Global Economy*, Report of the Premier's Council, Industrial Policy Studies, Vol. 3 (Toronto: Queen's Printer for Ontario, 1989)

Provincial Access Committee (British Columbia), *Access to Advanced Education and Job Training in British Columbia* (Victoria: Ministry of Advanced Education and Job Training, September 1988)

Psacharopoulos, George, *Future Trends and Issues in Education* (Ottawa: Economic Council of Canada, November, 1988)

Radwanski, George, *Ontario Study of the Relevance of Education, and the Issue of Dropouts* (Toronto: Ministry of Education, 1987)

Reich, Robert, *The Next American Frontier* (Middlesex, England and New York: Penguin, 1984)

Renewing the Commitment: How to Save General Education in Ontario Community Colleges (An unpublished brief submitted to Vision 2000 from General Education faculty at eight Ontario colleges, May 1989)

Report of the National Forum on Post-Secondary Education (Toronto: Council of Ministers of Education, Canada, 1988)

Royal Commission on Equality in Employment, *Equality in Employment* (Ottawa: Supply and Services Canada, 1984)

Rudin, S., *The Educational Needs and Interests of Senior Citizens in Metropolitan Toronto* (Toronto: George Brown College, 1987)

Science Council of Canada, "Winning in a World Economy: University-Industry Interaction and Economic Renewal in Canada," Report Number 39 (Ottawa: Supply and Services Canada, 1988)

Select Committee on Education, *Select Committee on Education: Report* ([Toronto]: Ontario Legislative Assembly: Select Committee on Education, December, 1988)

Senate Sub-Committee on Training and Employment, *In Training, Only Work Works* (Ottawa: Queen's Printer for Canada, December, 1987)

Senker, Peter, *Towards the Automatic Factory? The Need for Training* (Kempston, Bedford: IFS Publications, 1986)

Skills in Shortage 1989: A Survey of Selected Occupations in Metro Toronto, The Fifth Annual Report of the Metropolitan Toronto and York Region Labour Market and Training Needs Assessment (May, 1989)

Skolnik, Michael, "How Academic Program Review Can Foster Intellectual Conformity and Stifle Diversity of Thought and Method," *Journal of Higher Education*, Vol. 60, No. 6 (Ohio State University Press, 1988)

Skolnik, Michael L., "Some Unthinkable Options for Implementing the Entry to Practice Proposal for Nursing in Ontario — A View From Outside the Profession" (unpublished paper, Higher Education Group, OISE: University of Toronto, Toronto, 1988)

Social Assistance Review Committee, *Transitions* (Toronto: Ministry of Community and Social Services, 1988)

Sorge, Arndt and Wolfgang Streeck, "Industrial Relations and Technical Change: The Case for an Extended Perspective," in Richard Hyman and Wolfgang Streeck (ed.) *New Technology and Industrial Relations* (Oxford: Basil Blackwell, 1988)

Spenner, Kenneth I., "Technological Change, Skill Requirements and Education: The Case for Uncertainty," in Richard M. Cyert and David C. Mowery (ed.) *The Impact of Technological Change on Employment and Growth* (Cambridge, Massachusetts: Ballinger, 1988)

Stager, David A. A., *Focus on Fees — Alternative Policies for University Tuition Fees* (Toronto: Council of Ontario Universities, 1989)

Statistics Canada, *Canada's Women: A Profile of Their 1986 Labour Market Experience*, No. 71-205 (Ottawa: Supply and Services Canada, May 1988)

Statistics Canada, *Census Canada, 1986: Summary Tabulations of Labour Force, Mobility and Schooling* (Ottawa: Supply and Services Canada, March, 1988)

Statistics Canada, *Occupational Trends, 1961-1986*, 1986 Census, No. 93-151 (Ottawa: Supply and Services Canada, 1988)

Statistics Canada, *The Labour Force*, No. 71-001 (Ottawa: Supply and Services Canada, March 1989)

Stokes, N. and D. Foot, *Regional Differences in the Determinants of Post-Secondary Educational Choice in Canada: Community College versus University* (unpublished paper submitted to Vision 2000, Toronto, 1989)

Stoll, Robert and Elisabeth Scarff, *Student Attrition from Post-Secondary Programs at the Ontario Colleges of Applied Arts and Technology* (Toronto: Ministry of Colleges and Universities, 1983)

Student Success Taskforce, *Operational Documents* (Toronto: George Brown College, 1989)

Taskforce on Human Resource Development in the Third Decade, *A Blueprint Proposal for Human Resource Development in the Third Decade of the Ontario Colleges of Applied Arts and Technology* (Toronto, 1989)

Taskforce on Access to Professions and Trades in Ontario, *Access!* (Toronto: Ontario Ministry of Culture and Citizenship, 1989)

Task Force on Productivity Indices, *An Analysis of Unit Operating Costs in Ontario's Colleges of Applied Arts and Technology, 1978-79 to 1982-83* (Toronto: Ministry of Colleges and Universities, 1984)

Tinto, Vincent, "Dropout from Higher Education: A Theoretical Synthesis of Recent Research," *Review of Educational Research*, 45, No. 1, (1975), pp. 89-125

Wishard, William Van Dusen, *A World in Search of Meaning* (Washington, D.C., 1988)

Wismer, Susan, *Women's Education and Training in Canada*, (Toronto: Canadian Congress for Learning Opportunities for Women, 1988)

Wolfe, David, "Socio-Political Contexts of Technological Change: Some Conceptual Models," in Brian Elliott (ed.) *Technology and Social Process* (Edinburgh: Edinburgh University Press, 1988)

Yalnizyan, Armine, *Missing the Mark: Government Spending on Income Support and Training in Toronto* (Toronto: Social Planning Council of Metropolitan Toronto, 1988)

Yalnizyan, Armine and David Wolfe, *Target on Training: Meeting Workers' Needs in a Changing Economy* (Toronto: Social Planning Council of Metropolitan Toronto, 1989)

Zaharchuk, Ted and Jane Palmer, *A Report on Accreditation in the Colleges of Applied Arts and Technology* (Toronto: Decision Dynamics Corporation, 1978)

Zuboff, Shoshana, *In the Age of the Smart Machine: The Future of Work and Power* (New York: Basic Books, 1988)

E

Summary of Recommendations

Recommendation 1

The Government of Ontario and the Colleges of Applied Arts and Technology should adopt the following mandate for Ontario's colleges:

Preamble

Education has an essential role to play in the development of a world which is peaceful, environmentally sound, equitable and economically viable. Education should help to balance individual and community needs, and foster personal initiative and co-operation within human relationships based on mutual respect.

Education should give people the opportunity to develop the skills and knowledge they need to adapt to and make a constructive contribution to the world in which they live. Education should enhance students' choices and opportunities, and promote the development of individual potential. It should also assist learners in developing their commitment to social responsibility and care for the communities in which they live, and respect for cultural integrity and self-determination of those whose language and traditions may be different from their own.

It is the mandate of the Colleges of Applied Arts and Technology of Ontario:

To provide high-quality career education that enhances students' ability to acquire information, reason clearly, think critically, communicate effectively, apply their knowledge and participate in society as informed and productive citizens.

To make a college education as accessible as possible. Accessibility should include the opportunity to succeed, as well as the opportunity to enrol, and it must be provided in a way that achieves educational equity.

To be responsible, as a system, for quality assurance through system-wide standards and program review.

To work together and with other educational institutions to offer students opportunities for educational mobility and lifelong learning.

To create a dynamic, learner-driven system by anticipating and accommodating the diverse needs of students, both full-time and part-time, enrolled in credit and non-credit courses.

To forge partnerships in and with their communities, including employers, labour, community groups and governments.

To be participatory institutions in which decision-making involves both internal and external stakeholders.

To be model employers in the manner in which they invest in and manage human resource development, in their commitment to equity and in the creation of a positive, healthy and supportive working environment.

Recommendation 2

There should be a significant increase in the generic skills and general education content of programs leading to a college credential to ensure an equivalence of learning outcomes between these components and specific occupational skills.

Recommendation 3

There should be system-wide standards for all programs leading to a college credential. Such standards must focus on the learning outcomes expected of graduates from a program.

Recommendation 4

All programs leading to a college credential should be subject to regular, system-wide program review for the purposes of accreditation.

Recommendation 5

A College Standards and Accreditation Council (CSAC) should be established, with participation of internal and external stakeholders and with executive authority in the areas of system-wide program standards, review and accreditation.

Recommendation 6

Every college should have in place:

- educational equity policies and formally defined measures for implementing and monitoring those policies;
- race and ethnic relations policies to promote tolerance and understanding between peoples of different cultures and races;
- mechanisms to monitor employment equity policies to ensure that college personnel, boards and committees are representative of the diverse communities they serve; and
- mechanisms for building and maintaining effective partnerships with special communities and for advocating on their behalf on issues of educational equity.

Recommendation 7

The Ministry of Colleges and Universities should require every college board of governors to include in the college's annual report to the Minister a specific "Serving Communities" section outlining college activities in the areas of educational equity, race relations, employment equity and community outreach activities.

Recommendation 8

The Council of Regents should develop system-wide guidelines to assist colleges in developing educational equity policies. The Council should also produce and disseminate an annual report on college initiatives in serving communities.

Recommendation 9

Every college should, where necessary, conduct assessments of the literacy and numeracy levels of applicants to college credential programs for the purpose of appropriate placement. The need for assessment of an individual student should be at the discretion of the college.

Recommendation 10

Ontario's colleges should provide preparatory courses designed to meet the needs of those with a secondary school diploma or equivalent seeking admission to college credential programs. These courses may be offered in conjunction with local school boards.

Recommendation 11

The Ministry of Colleges and Universities should provide explicit funding to the colleges for preparatory courses in a manner consistent with the funding of college post-secondary programs.

Recommendation 12

The college system should continue to be a major provider of adult basic education.

Recommendation 13

The provincial government should accept responsibility for the co-ordination of policy, planning and increased funding of adult basic education programs in Ontario.

Recommendation 14

An ad hoc task force on fee-for-service training by colleges should be established by the Council of Regents to advise the Minister on policy guidelines which would foster the colleges' role in meeting the training needs of the existing workforce in a manner consistent with public policy goals.

Recommendation 15

Beginning from the current collective agreement, the parties should seek ways to facilitate the colleges' ability to provide fee-for-service activities.

Recommendation 16

Each college, in conjunction with faculty and staff, should develop strategies for establishing long-term relationships with local fee-for-service clients such as employers and labour organizations.

Recommendation 17

The Ontario government should adopt the principle that public funds, aimed at covering the costs associated with skills training, should be used primarily to support programs provided by or in conjunction with public institutions, including colleges.

Recommendation 18

In order to assure public accountability, any provincial body designated to foster more skills training should include employer and labour representatives and educators, and should produce a public, bi-annual report which:

- describes the training activities receiving public funds;
- shows the distribution of public funds (including federal funds allocated in Ontario) among the providers of training, be they public, private or joint activities;
- evaluates the effectiveness of such training, including an assessment of both quality and cost; and
- identifies training needs which are not being met and which require greater investment.

Recommendation 19

To better support the needs of part-time learners:

- every college should provide a variety of flexible learning opportunities, through varying educational methods, greater use of customized instructional methods, off-campus teaching locations, variable course entrance and completion dates, and other innovative approaches to delivery of relevant and adult-based programming for part-time learners;
- each college should have an advisory committee on part-time learning; and
- provincial funding and the internal allocation of college revenues should explicitly recognize the nature and importance of programs and services required by part-time learners.

 Recommendation 20

The government should establish the Prior Learning Assessment Network (PLAN), as recommended by the Task Force on Access to Professions and Trades in Ontario, with explicit inclusion of Ontario's colleges in the planning, implementation and operation of the system.

 Recommendation 21

The Ministry of Education, possibly through the newly formed Teacher Education Council of Ontario, should ensure that all teacher education programs (both pre-service and in-service) include components which furnish an in-depth knowledge of the educational services provided by the colleges. In particular, education about the colleges should be an explicit component of professional development for school guidance counsellors, teachers and principals.

 Recommendation 22

The Ministries of Education and Colleges and Universities should jointly establish a Provincial Schools/Colleges Co-ordinating Council, with representation of all relevant stakeholders from the secondary school and college systems, to improve school-college links and foster initiatives at the local level.

 Recommendation 23

The Minister of Colleges and Universities should endeavour to expand and improve the opportunities for students to move between the college and university sectors, while maintaining the distinctiveness of each sector.

 Recommendation 24

The college system should develop comprehensive programs of advanced training, on a selective basis, to address student needs. Graduates of such programs should receive a unique credential at the post-diploma level.

 Recommendation 25

The government should establish a provincial institute "without walls" for advanced training to:

- facilitate the development and co-ordination of arrangements between colleges and universities for combined college-university studies;
- offer combined college-university degree programs, with instruction based at and provided by colleges and universities; and
- recommend, where appropriate, to the College Standards and Accreditation Council the development of college-based programs of advanced training with a unique credential at the post-diploma level.

Recommendation 26

A formal agreement of association between the Institute and one or more Ontario universities should be established, providing for the associated universities to grant their degrees to graduates of programs conducted under the auspices of the Institute.

Recommendation 27

In the event that an agreement of association between the Institute and one or more universities cannot be reached within eighteen months, the government should vest degree-granting authority in the Institute itself.

Recommendation 28

A College System Strategic Planning Committee should be established by the Council of Regents. This standing committee would:

- undertake research on the quality-access-funding trade-offs facing Ontario's colleges;
- disseminate analyses and information across the college system; and
- recommend strategies to the Minister of Colleges and Universities for addressing trade-offs between quality, access and funding.

Recommendation 29

The Ministry of Colleges and Universities should review the structure of its funding to the colleges in order to provide a funding mechanism which:

- explicitly considers both access and quality;
- reduces counter-productive enrolment competition among the colleges;
- provides greater stability in the funding provided to each college by dampening the effects of enrolment changes on a college's grant; and
- continues to provide predictability and promote efficiency while strengthening accountability in the use of public resources.

Recommendation 30

The Ontario government should introduce a more participatory and co-ordinated system for developing government policies, initiatives, and funding arrangements affecting skills training provided by the colleges.

Recommendation 31

The government should initiate a study, encompassing both the college and university sectors, to assess the impact of alternative tuition fee and student assistance policies on access and institutional revenues.

Recommendation 32

The Council of Regents, through its Strategic Planning Committee, should develop and recommend a mechanism to co-ordinate information and plans relevant to the sharing of specialized resources among the colleges.

Recommendation 33

Every college's board of governors should reinforce Vision 2000's major objectives through its human resources planning by undertaking initiatives such as:

- setting clear budgetary targets for increasing the share of funds devoted to human resource development (HRD);

- including a section on HRD in the annual report to the Minister, which summarizes the college's progress in developing and implementing HRD policies and practices designed to achieve the objectives of the renewed mandate; and
- developing policy guidelines (to complement existing professional development leave policies) which provide regular opportunities and direct encouragement for external work experience, job exchanges or international activity for faculty, support staff and administrators.

Recommendation 34

The Ontario Government should work with all college stakeholders to establish and fund:
- a permanent Professional Development Fund to reinforce and expand upon the professional development efforts of the HRD in the Third Decade project; and
- an Instructional Development Task Force to provide leadership in helping the colleges develop learner-centred curriculum and alternative delivery.

Recommendation 35

The Minister of Colleges and Universities should provide sufficient funding to enable an Ontario university (or several, working in a consortium) to develop graduate-level programs for community college personnel.

Recommendation 36

The colleges should work together to introduce effective means for fostering applied scholarship as a way of enhancing the primacy of the colleges' teaching function.

Recommendation 37

Each college should experiment in developing reciprocal methods of performance review which are formative in nature for all employees. The process for developing these procedures should itself be collaborative in nature.

Recommendation 38

Each college's board of governors should further develop its capacity for strategic planning, especially on issues related to quality, access and funding, and for working in partnership with a range of stakeholders to meet student needs.

Recommendation 39

The Council of Regents should conduct an operational review of its board appointment responsibilities, employing a third-party process.

Recommendation 40

The Minister of Colleges and Universities should establish a Vision 2000 Implementation Committee to co-ordinate evaluation and development of detailed plans for implementation of Vision 2000's recommendations. This committee should involve all of the major constituencies, both internal and external, that participated in Vision 2000.